Well it was fun...

Ann Stanmore

Preface

This book has been written mainly for my son Ian and other members of the family, not least my late sister Shirley's children, Debbie, Louisa, Helen and Antony, and maybe it will also brighten someone's day. It is a light hearted account of my fun growing up in the forties and part of the fifties. This is a series of anecdotes from my earliest memory until I embark on a new chapter in my life at fifteen.

While all of the mini adventures are totally true and really did happen as stated, the actual venues etc may have become a little blurred round the edges due to the passage of time and a memory that is a little worn now!! For example, I mention a back yard in one tale, and while I remember the house clearly and most definitely the tale, the actual yard is a little vague. I was after all, only five at the time!

My parents, both now deceased, were fun loving, happy people, as was my sister Shirley, who was born five years after me, and is unfortunately, now deceased. My dad lived by the maxim that if he had made someone smile that day, it had been worth getting up for. He passed this on to me and my sister and if by this book I can make you, the reader, have a little chuckle, then dad would have been proud.

My thanks to both my parents for spreading their happiness around. I hope a little has rubbed off on me. Only the reader can judge.

Before I begin to tell about my adventures while growing up, I had better tell a little about me. I was born in March 1940 in a hospital in Winchester. My parents were living in Andover at the time, but due to hospitals being full up with war wounded soldiers, Mum was taken to Winchester for my birth.

Not long after that, my parents returned to their native Leicestershire. We lived at various address's in Leicestershire, and also at several others, including time spent in Lancashire, Oxfordshire and finally in Berkshire. Apart from the time he considered himself a business man, my Dad would see another job as a proof reader advertised, a bit better than the current one was and we would up sticks and move to somewhere else. In those days, many jobs had houses to go with them, called 'tied' houses, and if you left the job you left the house. I wasn't always happy to say goodbye to my friends, but actually came to enjoy meeting new people and seeing how others lived in different parts of the country. I also learnt how to deal with sometimes having the mickey taken at school when my accent would be different. Something I was able to change eventually so wherever I was, I could speak with the same accent. I learnt very early how to adapt to new circumstances and environments, and I think this has been very helpful during my life, maybe (I like to believe) making me into a more understanding person.

One

Oh how I loved my dollies pram, all shining and bright
My Mum and Dad they worked so hard, to make it just right
It was an old and broken thing when Dad first spotted it
They made it to be really nice and where my doll could sit

Why wasn't it new, do I hear you ask
Well really that was a difficult task........................

My earliest childhood memory was probably one of receiving a birthday present when I was three years old. I don't remember having a birthday party that year. I would imagine there was too much going on with the war at that time for my parents to think about birthday parties.

What I do remember oh, so clearly, was the present I had from my Mum and Dad. It was a dolls pram. This might not seem terribly exciting, but to me it was the most beautiful thing. I was spellbound! I didn't know anybody who had one. I didn't realise at the time, but this was because of the war.

It didn't matter to me that it wasn't new, in fact I don't think that registered in my young mind. I was later told that you couldn't buy a new dolls pram for love nor money (well maybe if you were rich!!) because it wasn't a commodity that was being produced during those bleak war days.

I learnt later, when I was older, that my Dad had found it in a lady's cellar when he emptied her gas meter (I explain about Dad working as a gas man later on). It had only three wheels, the hood wouldn't stay up, and the lining was ripped! Plus it was dirty from being in the cellar for years.

Luckily for me, my Dad saw the potential here and asked the lady how much she wanted for it. He explained that he wanted to do it up for his little daughter for her birthday.

The kind lady wouldn't take anything for it, she said she would be pleased for him to take it away. Dad since told me, he bore that pram away, balancing it on his bike, the happiest man alive because he would be able to give me a nice present.

Looking at it then, so I have been told, you would never imagine it would turn out to be such a lovely pram.

When I was fast asleep in bed, Dad worked on repairing and doing it up. He was able to replace all the wheels, so it had four good ones, repaired the lining and mended the hood. Then Mum scrubbed it inside out and finally Dad painted the bodywork.

The finishing touch was the bedding Mum made. A frilly little pillow, sheet on the bottom, blanket and a pretty cover. One of my grandmas gave me a new dolly with clothes she had knitted and oh my goodness, was I ever a happy little girl.

That pram gave me so much joy and was played with many, many times for the next few years. Such a lot a little girl can pretend with when she has a dolls pram, I had a vivid imagination which was used to it's full extent with that dolls pram.

What love had gone into my beautiful present. Worth much, much more than something bought from a shop. It was only when

I got older that I really appreciated all the things my parents did for me when I was growing up.

The first few years of my life were very difficult ones for everyone and there were many sacrifices my parents made for me. By the time my sister was born, things were beginning to get a little easier although it took several years after the war finished for there to be a semblance of 'normal' life again.

It shows what can be done with determination, effort and most of all, love.

Money and goods were scarce in those war years, but, at least in our house, there was never a shortage of love.

Two

My Dad he was a lovely man, he always made me smile
He would take me on his bike, and for a little while
I'd sit upon his crossbar and keep my legs out wide
We'd look out for the policeman, is he coming up the side

The policeman played a great big drum in the village band
He'd bang it really hard, the drumstick in his hand
If you went out Sunday morn, he always could be seen
Banging on his big old drum on the village green

Read on and you will not fail
To hear about this little tale................

If the weather was fine, Dad would take me out on his push-bike. This was a real delight for me, and I would be so excited when I knew we were going out. At first we didn't have a seat for me, so I sat on the crossbar with instructions from Dad to stick my legs out so they were away from the spokes. I understood that we were being naughty because we really should have had a seat for me, but Dad explained that there were varying degrees of naughtiness and this wasn't one of the bad ones. However, he did tell me he would get a seat for me as soon as they had enough money for one.

It wasn't until I was grown up that I realised the importance of these bike rides. Mum and Dad tried to take me out as much as possible because the living conditions where we were at that time were pretty appalling. We had a back yard area that was used by all the houses in the terrace and had toilets (or privvies as we called them) in a row at the end of the yard. Each house had their own but they were horrible places and had to be emptied because there was no flush toilets there then. Some people had flush toilets. My Grandma Bramley did, and it was lovely when we went to her house to go to a nice, light and clean place where you pulled a chain and it all went away! My Grandma Ratcliffe didn't have this luxury unfortunately, we had to go down the garden there but it was nicer than the one we had in that yard, where although each family had their own, some people would use any one.

Dad also used to take me when I was a little older, to watch Loughborough playing football on a Saturday afternoon. I loved this and sometimes, if it was crowded and I couldn't see, Dad would lift me up on his shoulders. I didn't really understand the rules of the game then, just knew our side had to score goals, but it was being out with my Dad that was great. The fact that we were watching Loughborough Brush was secondary!

Anyway, back to this tale. We would go out into the countryside and find a nice green area and play ball. I loved sitting there as we whizzed along the road. Dad would show me the little wild flowers and we would listen to the birds singing. It was a magical time for me and I loved every minute. Being out with my Dad was really the best thing ever. Dad always made things funny and we used to laugh a lot. He was still doing this when he was an old man in a nursing home. All the nurses used to be in stitches. However, back to the story......

Well, in the meantime, I had instructions to keep my eyes open for the village bobby. As mentioned earlier, this gentleman played in the village band in his spare time and could be seen on Sundays in the bandstand on the park playing his drum. Once he was playing in the band with his big drum out in the street. I think it was a march for something and the band was going down the high street. Anyway, he spotted Dad with me on his bike and put down his drum and chased us down the road waving his drum-stick at us!! Dad would be laughing and I started to giggle. Oh my naughty Dad, how I loved you.

Actually, I found out later that Dad and the policeman were friends, but he couldn't let Dad off without making it known he disapproved of his actions. Thankfully, it wasn't long before I was sitting on a proper bike seat but secretly, I was a bit disappointed! Nothing like being naughty with your Dad's approval.

It really isn't surprising that one of my favourite things even when I was fully grown up, married and had children of my own, was riding my bike. In fact, it was only arthritis that made me stop when I was in my forties. Something I miss. I would bike for miles and miles. There is a special kind of freedom cycling along the country roads, I never tired of it. Sometimes when I see a dad with a son or daughter cycling down the road, I remember those magical times.

See what you started Dad!!

Lots of fun was had when I learnt to ride my first bike but that's another story in another part of this book.

Three

A long time ago a lady looked up and saw a little girl
So high above the ground, you could hardly see her curl
Oh goodness me, she said in fear, she might be going to fall
I'd better get her down so it doesn't happen at all

What happened next, was her fate sealed?
Read on my friend, all is revealed..................

It had been another warm day and it was coming to an end for me, as my Mum got me ready for bed. I didn't want to go because I didn't think I was tired and so why couldn't I still play. I thought you went to bed when you were tired and so went to sleep!! Cruel world when you are only four years old! So off to bed I went. I hated going up the stairs because they were very narrow and there was a door at the bottom which was always closed. On the other hand, it was my very own little world when the door was closed. I could creep out of bed and if I was quiet, nobody would know.

Mostly though, I was always a little bit afraid up there, especially in the winter when it was dark when I went to bed. Some nights I would lie awake, determined not to sleep until the light came on when my parents came to bed. Only when I saw the sliver of light under my bedroom door could I relax and go to sleep. I now know that had I told either Mum or Dad of my fear, they would have reassured me and maybe have left a light on the stairs on until I had gone to sleep, but I had too much pride to let on I was scared. That would have been dreadful in my eyes, to show I was afraid was not to be thought of!

However, life can be very exciting when you are little! Well, as I said earlier, it had been a warm day and was now a warm evening. It was still daylight so I wasn't scared and I lay down in bed, Mum kissed me goodnight and went downstairs. When I heard the door at the bottom of the stairs close, I opened my eyes. I had a book at the bedside I could look at if I wanted to. I wouldn't get told off for that. This particular night, I didn't want to look at my book. I could read a lot of the words but tonight I didn't feel like it.

So I sat up in bed and wondered what to do. I looked across at the window and saw clouds in the sky moving very slowly and thought I would have a better look. I very quietly crept out of bed and went to the window to have a look at the clouds. The wind was gently blowing the curtain and I stood on tiptoe to see if I could see anything underneath the window. We didn't have a garden and you could see into the next street. Well, I couldn't see the street very well, I mean at four years old, of course I couldn't, I was very tiny.

OK I thought, let's get a better look and tried to climb up onto the window ledge, but realised I needed something to stand on. There was a chair in the corner of my bedroom, and I carefully dragged this to the window. Right, now I could climb on the chair and get onto the window ledge.

Oh this was much better, I was swinging my legs in time with the breeze blowing gently. I could see lots and lots of stuff, the houses in the next street, and the smoke coming out of the chimneys! It was funny watching it go up into the sky and I was nearly as high as the chimney pots wow! I could even see the pub on the corner with people going in and out. One man came outside with a pint of beer in his hand.

I saw a lady going down the street and waved to her. She didn't wave back though, but she said something and I couldn't hear her. So I forgot about her and carried on swinging my legs and enjoying myself, daydreaming away.

I didn't hear Mum coming in my room. Oh dear, what had I done!! My Mum was being very cross with me and she made me go back to bed.

I couldn't understand why Mum was so upset. I mean, I didn't think I had been naughty! I realised then she thought I would fall out of the window, the lady in the street had knocked on our door and told my Mum what I was doing. What a spoilsport!! It was lovely and of course I wouldn't fall. I told my Mum, I had both my hands on the side of the window and therefore I wouldn't fall!! Honestly, grown ups!!

Four

At five years old you have no fear
It soon becomes so very clear
You want to see what's over there
Then go and look, it's only fair

You have to learn what's going on
So what you do is start to run
And go in through an open door
It's asking for trouble I'm sure................

The house we lived in when I was five years old was in Freehold Street in Loughborough and had a factory opposite. This actually was a bell foundry where bells were made for all over the world. The bell foundry came to Loughborough in 1839 and is still there. It is the largest bell foundry in the world and many famous bells have been made there. The largest bell in Britain, the Great Tom at St Paul's Cathedral in London, was cast there in 1881.

Now when I was five I didn't know much about all this. I only knew there were some very big bells in there. I had seen when the doors opened for people to go in and out. This was an absolute fascination to me and having a vivid imagination, well! You can see what my problem was..........I just had to see properly. Mum and Dad had said bells were made there and that was all I knew.

Of course I knew I shouldn't go across the road, I was only allowed in the yard outside the back. This was a yard for all of the houses in our block and I didn't like it very much. Some of the people who lived near us weren't very nice and even as a five year old, I realised they were not like us. I thought some of them were quite dirty and Mum had said not to play with the children of one family. So I spent quite a bit of time looking out into the road at the front and became fascinated with the bell foundry.

When we went to church I would listen to the bells ringing and wonder if they came from the bell foundry across the road.

The people of Loughborough were very familiar with bells because we had the famous Carillon there. The Loughborough Carillon was the first grand Carillon in Britain. A Carillon is a musical instrument, not a "peal of bells" more familiar in many English Churches. Loughborough's Carillon is based on 47 bells and follows the tradition of Belgian bell music. In a Carillon the bells are rung by forcing a clapper down onto the bell from levers at a keyboard, or clavier. The Carillonneur therefore plays the music which can be enjoyed across the surrounding Queens Park and well beyond.

The Carillon Tower was built as a War Memorial by public subscription in memory of the 480 men of the town who fell in the Great War as inscriptions on the Bells testify. Bronze tablets on the exterior of the Tower commemorate the fallen of both World Wars and subsequent conflicts.

Of course, I knew nothing of all this when I was small, I just knew I liked bells and wanted to see over the road.

Obviously by now you have guessed the next part of this story...............of course I had to go over there somehow. It is surprising how crafty you can be when you are little (have I ever changed??).

One day, Mum was busy with my baby sister and when I said "can I go out to play please" she said yes. Now I knew I was supposed to stay in the back yard, and went out there. I also knew if you went down an ally nearby it would take you to the road outside the front of the house. What was on the other side of the road? Of course the bell foundry. My perfect chance! So I checked nobody was watching me and over the road I went. Now I had to get inside the foundry itself without anyone seeing me. I know I was only five but I knew I would be in trouble if I was caught.

Then I saw it! A side door that someone hadn't closed properly....perfect! So I simply went in! I was amazed at what I saw. Bells that were bigger than our house!! Or that's how they seemed to me! There were some tiny ones as well, but it was the big ones I couldn't take my eyes from.

It was very noisy in there and I didn't like that much, but oh all those bells! I could have gazed at them forever and ever! I just wanted to stand there looking at them. I was a bit scared really, some were so big. Unfortunately (or from a grown ups point of view, fortunately) I was spotted by one of the men working there. Oh what a hue and cry!! I wasn't touching anything, only looking albeit open mouthed and wide eyed! One man was very nice and came and talked to me. I told him I just wanted to see the bells.

The next minute, Mum appeared on the scene and I was hurried back home. Why do all the good things have to stop so soon? Oh well, at least I had seen what it was like over the road! The mystery was solved.

There was something that happened when we lived in Freehold Street, my sister caught Whooping Cough. Shirley was only a tiny little baby, she must have only have been a few weeks old at the time. I didn't understand what it was, but I just knew she couldn't get her breath properly.

Mum frightened me very much when one day, Shirley was struggling to breathe and Mum picked her up and held her upside down and was patting her back! I didn't know what she was doing, I thought she was hurting my baby sister!! However, Mum did explain when Shirley was breathing alright again, that it was a way of helping her get her breath. Scary stuff, didn't think I wanted to be a mummy.

One other thing that happened at this time was the end of World War Two. As I was only five in 1945, I only have hazy memories of this. However, I do remember that all the grown-ups were very happy and planned to hold street parties to celebrate. I remember all the trestle tables with lots of food on in the road, and someone wheeled a piano out so everyone had a good old sing song.

Obviously I didn't realise the significance of the party, but remember running round the tables and nobody told me off!! I think everyone was too happy to bother about me playing around! I think I must have been very late to bed that night, because I can remember it was really dark outside and people had their doors open with lights on, to help illuminate outside.

I wish now I had asked my parents more about this time when I was older. Sadly it is too late now.

Loughborough Carillon

Five

It was probably just as well, I had to go to school
My curiosity channelled as I had to follow the rule
I went to my grandma's each day for my dinner
Which as you will see, wasn't always a winner..........................

When I first started school, Mum worked in the Food Office at the Town Hall. Previously, before the war began, Mum worked as a bookbinder in a printing firm, which is where she met my Dad. As it was during the war years, although soon war was to end, Mum had the job of issuing Ration Books. My Dad was refused permission to go in the forces on health grounds and instead worked emptying gas meters until war ended. He was also a Fire Marshall. Dad's real job was as a proof reader, which he returned to when war ended.

Mum used to put me on the bus to go to school, and the bus conductor was supposed to look after me until my stop. I bitterly resented this as even though I was so very young, I was fiercely independent. I knew what to do, I didn't need anybody telling me. That was my reasoning!

Anyway, because my grandmother (Grandma Bramley) lived in Herrick Road which was near to the school and Mum would be at work anyway, it was arranged I would go there for my dinner. How different life was then. Not only did I travel on the bus on my own, I went home to grandma's for dinner on my own. (We all seemed to do this. How times have changed).

So back to the story......I loved my grandma and liked going to her house but, and this is a big but, I hated having dinner there. I understood in later years how difficult it was to produce a tasty meal during the days of rationing. Such small amounts of meat were allowed, nobody could afford to waste anything (today's recycling is really history). It was quite common to have stews that consisted of a tiny amount of meat and lots of vegetables with of course dumplings if you were lucky. Yes, it sounds good doesn't it. Not if you were five and went to grandma's it wasn't. All of the meat allocated for the stew would go in. That included all the fat and gristle!! I would be in trouble if I didn't eat it all and many a battle would reign during those lunchtimes. Poor gran! I must have given her hell!!

There was one day when I had had this awful stew and managed to eat most of the fat and gristle (ugh), and pudding was dished up. Now, I had discovered when I started school, I didn't like milk. It made me feel sick to drink it and there were many battles with teachers over this until Mum intervened. So in the light of this, you can understand my feelings when Grandma put rice pudding in front of me! Not only was it made with my dreaded liquid, it was a lot of milk and not much rice! Well, I sat there and stirred and played around with it for ages. Gran was getting cross with me because she insisted I eat it before I could get down. Now this was terrible for me because my much older cousin had arrived. He was in the army and was home on leave after fighting in the war. I loved him dearly and was longing to go into the garden where he had promised to push me on my swing before I went back to school.

I could see him through the French windows and so wanted to get out there. Grandma came back into the dining room (she had long since finished her dinner) and said would I eat it with a little jam on and duly plonked a spoonful of jam in the middle of the rice pudding. By this time it had got cold and the milk was congealing at the edges. I watched the jam sink into the middle and thought what am I going to do. I can't possibly eat that!

Now my grandparents had a nice house with nice furniture and the dining chairs were fancy and had knobs on each side at the top. All of a sudden, I just picked up the bowl of congealed mess and upturned it on one of the knobs!!! I was actually horrified at what I had done. Whatever made me do that? I wasn't usually a naughty girl. Why had I been so stupid, whatever would Grandma say? I can picture it even to this day, the bowl upside down and rice, milk and jam running down the back of the chair onto the carpet!!!

I will say no more about this episode except to say I never did get to go on my swing with my cousin pushing me, but I never ate the rice pudding either!

On my swing on a happier day!

When I first used to go to Grandma Bramley's for dinner from school. I used to love playing with her dog Paddy. He was a lovely brown and white springer spaniel. I would play with Paddy every-day when I had eaten my dinner before going back to school.

We played together every day for almost a year and then, the unthinkable happened! Paddy bit me! I couldn't believe it. Why did he do it? I remember being very scared. Also of course, I was bleeding and in pain. Paddy had bitten me on the side of my nose very close to my eye.

Grandma bathed my nose and took me to the lady a couple of doors away, who was a nurse. It was decided I needn't go to the hospital and certainly didn't need to see the doctor. It would heal on it's own in time. So I even went straight off to school! Mind you, I was the centre of attention all afternoon.

The sad thing about it was that Grandma gave Paddy away (he wasn't destroyed, because it was assumed I was over playful, which is almost certainly true). The other thing to develop from this, is that I am still even now, a little bit nervous of dogs and would never have one myself.

Six

This naughty little girl you've met, wasn't always so
She could be good as well as bad and as she did know
If she'd been good her Mum would tell a story before bed
Her Dad would do the very same it really should be said

And so a love of books and words was sown
Which over the years has grown and grown
That little girl has also grown and look
She is now writing her very own book................

As we were growing up, one of the highlights of our childhood was stories at bedtime from either Mum or Dad. They both had very different styles which I now believe reflected their individual personalities. My sister and I loved both types of stories and there was no trouble getting ready for bed if we thought there would be a story.

We would get all ready and be in our nighties and would go and sit downstairs by the fire if it was winter time. This was the best time for us for stories because the fire played an important part. We took turns in picking one thing each and then whoever was telling the story would pick a third. We picked these by looking at the flames and saying what we thought something was. I might see a house, my sister might see a flower. I think our parents would have picked something they wanted to tell a story about!! So the three items were worked into a story.

Mum's stories were the conventional, nice story where good triumphed over evil. There was nothing scary in Mum's tales, but they were always 'safe' where you knew it would be alright in the end and the good children always won over the bad ones. We always felt sort of comfortable with them.

Now Dad's were a totally different sort. You were always excited and you never knew what would happen next. You were never sure if the good people would win or not. In short they were exciting! Not sure if they were always the right sort before bed but we loved them.

Another thing Dad would do was serialise his stories sometimes. I would often go to bed trying to think what would happen next in the current story. I am sure this must have had an impact on my behaviour in the day, because if I was naughty I would be sent to bed early and wouldn't get to hear the story that night!!

Very rarely did my parents actually read to either my sister or myself from books, preferring to tell their own stories. (This is something I continued with my own children). We were very fortunate that both our parents had wonderful imaginations, and made stories alive for us.

We were encouraged to read as much as possible. In my case I took that on board a little more than was meant, indeed I was actually told off for reading too much!! I would read all my Christmas books before the end of the Christmas holidays. I would read anything I could get my hands on.

My Mum's mum, my Grandma Bramley, was very religious and was a Methodist. This meant when I went to stay with her, if it was a Sunday, I wouldn't be allowed to read a newspaper (something I did avidly at home). Sundays at Grandma and Grandad's house were devoted to going to church, which we walked to once in the morning and again for the evening service.

We had to do everything quietly in the time between church and what we were allowed to do was very limited. I would get bored on those days and I would then be allowed to read a Missionary magazine that we got from the church. Actually this was really interesting and for a period of my life, I wanted to be a missionary!

Now at home, we were allowed to read anything on a Sunday, Mum and Dad were not strict on that at all.

We never had any money, but were indeed very happy and never felt we missed out on anything. Only once did I have a twinge of resentment and that was one Christmas. My best friend Margaret, said she was getting a paint box for Christmas and I asked my parents could I please have one as well. They gave the traditional answer of 'wait and see'. Christmas morning dawned and sure enough, there was a lovely big box of paints. I took them to school and my friend took hers. I learnt then to hide my feelings because my friend's paint box had drawers in underneath with tubes of paint as well as the pallets on the top and the whole thing was made of wood! Mine, although large, was nothing like hers and was only tin, I never told Mum and Dad and sincerely hope my disappointment didn't show. Also I don't think Margaret ever knew how I envied her at that moment.

Both my sister and I loved April Fool's Day when we were children. Dad would make it so funny. He would send a letter to us with 'April Fool' written in. We would have boiled eggs and when you cracked the top you would find it was an empty shell!! Then Mum would give us real ones, but they were special because she would have coloured them and sometimes drew faces on. As the years went by, we knew these things would happen and never tired of them. We would look forward to them and wonder if Dad had thought of a new trick to play!

Dad used to make us laugh a lot and my friends used to come round because Dad always made them laugh as well. A favourite of Dad's was if Mum asked him to put the kettle out he would go into the kitchen and literally put the kettle outside!! Then say, 'oh I'm sorry, I thought that was what you meant!'

I really can't remember all the funny things he did, but we always seemed to be laughing. Dad never changed on this, the whole of his life he was the same. Even in the nursing home before he died, he would have the nurses in stitches. If someone gave him a cake he would say, 'oh that's lovely will you cut it in half and I'll have both ends'.

He would also tease us at mealtimes. If Mum brought a pudding in to the table, Dad would say, 'oh thank you dear, what is everyone else going to have?' So many wonderful memories!

I remember my sister and I had to wear liberty bodices. These were awful things and we both hated them as did all my friends. We would have to wear vests first which was fine, but then these awful things called liberty bodices had to go on top. They were a sleeveless v-necked thick garment with rubber buttons down the front. They were supposed to keep us warm, which of course they did, but we didn't care about that. I hated it when I had a bath and my fingers were wrinkly from the bath and I couldn't do up the stupid rubber buttons!

When Shirley was old enough to go to school, there were so many arguments with her and Mum, because Shirley flatly refused to wear it and of course, Mum insisted she did. If she could get away with it, Shirley would disappear and take it off, but Mum always found out and then it was trouble! By the way, I never told on her!!

When I think back, I suppose they did make sense at the time, because we didn't go to school or anywhere else in a car, always we had to walk. When we got to school they weren't the warm centrally heated places they are now, so I imagine we would have been even colder without those dreaded liberty bodices!

There was one other thing I remember my sister doing and that was wearing a bonnet with ribbons tied round the tie bit of the bonnet! Because at that time, nits and lice etc were very prevalent, soldiers used to come home from the war fields with them, and we were checked rigorously for any nits. In view of this, Mum wouldn't allow us to have long hair. Now plaits were very common at that time and Shirley so desperately wanted long hair so she could have plaits.

Oh dear, more arguments now, long hair or not! It was a definite no from Mum. When you grow up you can have it how you like, she would tell us. So Shirley wasn't going to be outdone. Whenever we were at home, she would put a bonnet on her head (bonnets were another very common item of clothing then) but didn't tie the ends under her chin. Instead she tied a ribbon round each and let them swing, pretending she had plaits. Another thing we laughed about when we were grown up.

Sister Shirley

Seven

Oh the magic of the Eastern girls, with jugs upon their head
Appealed to me when I was young and read my book in bed
One day I acted out the part, and did I cause a fright
When I arrived at home to mum, I really looked a sight

What did I do? I'll let you know
To find out more just read below................

It was a beautiful morning when I woke up and I jumped out of bed and tried to be quiet because it seemed like it was early and I didn't want to wake my little sister up. When she woke up I wouldn't get any peace, she would want me to play with her and she was too little.

So down the stairs I crept, but guess what? Of course, Mum was already up and the kettle was boiling for my cocoa. I hated tea then because Mum made me have it milky and I didn't like milk. I wasn't allowed coffee as I was too young, but cocoa I could have and that was lovely. It's little wonder these days, I prefer my tea with only a dash of milk. I wonder if a psychologist would say it was my way of getting my own back??

Anyway, I digress. I had my cocoa and some porridge. I liked porridge if it was Three Bears and no other. I discovered when I was grown up that if Mum couldn't get Three Bears she would tip the other brand into a Three Bears box and I would eat it ok. I guess times haven't changed that much because I suspect Mums today do similar things.

It wasn't a school day, so I was looking forward to going out to play. We had moved house since the bell foundry incident and now lived in the same town in a road called Parklands Drive but it was nicer, we were nearly in the country. There were fields and a stream near where we lived and best of all, lots of trees to climb. By the time I had had my breakfast, my sister had got up. Yes, she wanted me to play with her!! So I did for a while because she was quite sweet, but I soon became bored playing baby games (Shirley was after all 5 years younger), so I asked Mum if I could go out to play. She said I could but she wanted to make a treacle tart for pudding that day and had run out of treacle, so would I first go to the shop and get some for her.

I didn't really want to because it was turning out to be a really hot day and I wanted to get out and call for my friends, but I didn't tell Mum that because I knew she had a lot to do and I did love treacle tart. So off I went to the shop. Now when I was young where we lived the nearest shop was about a mile and a half away. By the time I came out of the shop, I was getting all hot and bothered.

What can I do to pass the time on a quite long walk back home I thought to myself. Aha, I've got it! The Eastern ladies carried big pots on their heads with one hand on their hips. I could do that with this tin of treacle!! So, I straightened up my glasses that were slipping a bit because I was hot, and plonked the treacle tin on my head. Off I went, enjoying myself now, imagining I was living in the East and trying to sway my hips like I had seen in pictures.

Oh this is great, I thought to myself and arrived back home eventually. All was well until as Mum opened the back door for me, I lifted the tin down from my head. Shock, horror .... oh goodness me!! I had put the tin upside down and when I lifted it off the lid stayed on my head and all the treacle ran through my hair, down my glasses and all over the place. It had melted in the heat and was all runny. Mum stood there gob-smacked for a minute. She said later she didn't know whether to laugh or cry, smack me or hug me!!! Anyway, I was rather unceremoniously dumped in the bath and never got any treacle tart that day.

Eight

There was a little girl, who really could be bad
She lost the ration book, and made her Mum so sad
She was sent down to the shops one day
And coming home she stopped to play

She saw some friends she knew, who were playing a game
Well naturally she wanted to, do the very same
She put down on the floor, the shopping and the book
And played a game of marbles, but when she went to look

The precious ration book was gone
To see what happed then, read on………………………..

During the war years, as older readers will remember, people were issued with ration books allocating what food and how much you could buy. As there were so many away fighting the war, there wasn't so much food produced and what was had to be rationed out so everyone got something.

Ration books were a very precious commodity in those days, because without them you couldn't buy any food.

One thing we had a lot of was rabbit. I had some uncles who would go out shooting and bring back rabbits which were shared around the family. These were sometimes roasted and we did have it at Christmas one year I remember. Rabbit stew was another thing and I liked this. There was no fat and gristle on that but we did have to look out for buckshot!!

Well one day, my Mum sent me (again!! I felt sure I spent my life running errands! However, I realised in later years she had not long had a baby - there were five years between my sister and me) down to the shops for some groceries. Of course, I had to take the ration book with me. It was a lovely sunny day (were all the days sunny when I was little???), and I didn't mind going down to the shops. Running a message was what we called it. Doesn't make grammatical sense does it, but that's what we said.

Anyway, off I went and bought the things Mum had asked for, pleased with myself that I had got everything right. So to go home with the goods........aha, that's when trouble stepped in!!

I saw a bunch of my friends playing marbles. Well I absolutely loved marbles and never went anywhere without some in my pocket (funny all my dresses had pockets in, very handy!). So what more natural than I stopped to have a game. I said to my friends I mustn't be long because I had to get the shopping home to Mum, but I would have a little go.

Wow, I lost a few games, then started to win. I know how gamblers must feel, because once I had started, I couldn't stop!!

I have no idea now how long I played, but when I suddenly realised it must be too long and I should get home, I looked for the shopping and the ration book. Oh dear, I felt so bad when I found out that the shopping was still there, but the ration book had gone!!!

Oh dear, what to do??? Mum would flay me alive (I had no idea what that meant, but I had heard someone say it, and it sounded right for this occasion). My friends and I searched everywhere. We had been playing on a grass verge at the roadside, so anyone could have come and taken it.

Eventually, I made my sorry little way home and confessed as soon as I got there. Oh dear!! I didn't get punished in any usual sense, but to see my Mum so distraught was worse than any hiding! I felt so bad, I think I punished myself with such sorrow at what I had done.

All turned out well in the end, because my grandmother helped Mum out with some food until she could get a replacement ration book. Oh boy, did I learn the lesson to finish one thing before doing another!! Never to be forgotten.

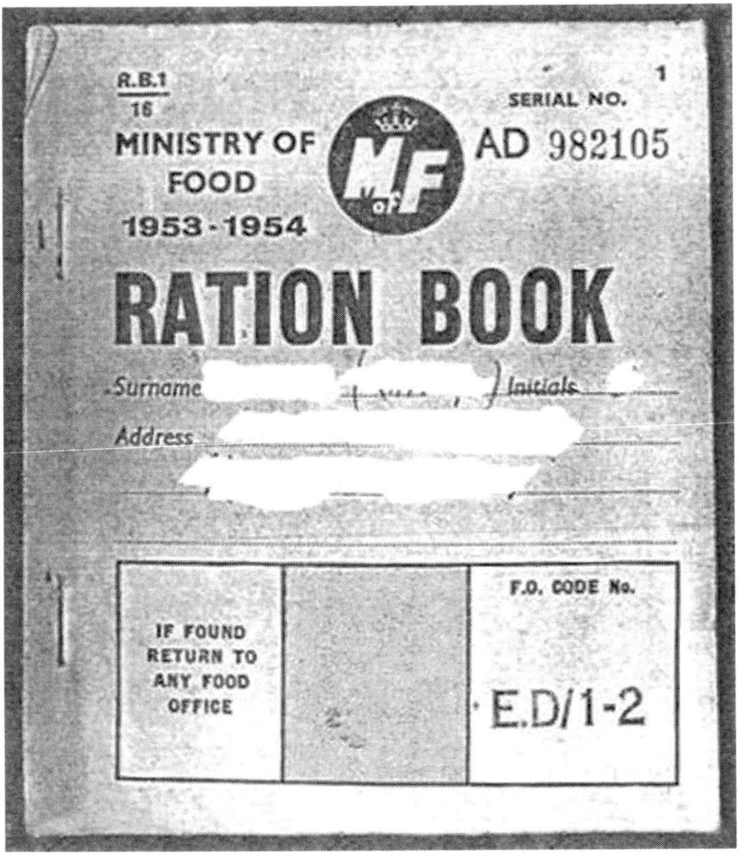

Example of Ration Book

Nine

I know I had a lovely Mum, we laughed a lot together
But she would send me down the shop in all kinds of weather
There was a consolation, it really should be said
When I was sent down there to buy, a crusty loaf of bread...............

There were many times I would have to go to the shops for my Mum when my sister was a baby. I understand now that it would have been a hassle for Mum to go. She would have to get my sister ready and then walk quite a long way to the shop and with the knowledge that I could run there and back quite quickly I can now see why it was me that had to go. I think I ran everywhere when I was little. I always wanted to get things done or see what was going on, there didn't seem time to mess about, too much to see and do. However, it wasn't unknown for me to dawdle!

Actually unless I was wanting to play with my friends, I didn't really mind going to the shop for Mum because there was always something to look at on the way. We didn't see many cars in those days and I only went in one once a year when we would go on holiday. Dad would get a taxi to take us to the railway station. That was as exciting as going on holiday itself. Some of my friends had never been in a car and it was a source of conversation for weeks after we came home.

What I used to like to do on my trip to the shops, was investigate things in the hedge. There were some really big hedges along the side of the road to the shop and sometimes you would find birds nesting. I got to know where they would nest and used to try to see if there were any eggs in there (and no, I didn't collect eggs although I knew some big boys that did).

Some parts of the hedges were of hawthorn and it was a popular thing to do to eat the 'bread and cheese' leaves. My friends and I used to do this on our way to school in the mornings. It's a wonder those hawthorns survived our daily onslaught. You would think our parents never fed us!! It was also nice to see if there were any new flowers arrived since I last looked. As I looked almost every day, I sometimes had a long wait!!

I also passed two of my friends houses on the way to the shop and sometimes I would call for one of them to see if they wanted to go with me. We could always chatter away nineteen to the dozen and giggled ourselves silly. They weren't always home or sometimes if they were their mums might not let them out. They might have been naughty and so kept in or it might be their mealtime.

The time I didn't really mind so much going to the shop, was if Mum wanted bread. Now the strange thing here is that at tea time at home, I didn't like eating the crusts on my bread. Mum couldn't use the familiar expression 'they will make your hair curly' because mine already was! So, while I hated crusts on my sandwiches, when I had to buy a fresh loaf for Mum, well I simply couldn't resist nibbling the corners off the lovely, warm, freshly baked loaf when I was carrying it home. I was told off so many times and always promised I wouldn't do it this time, my good intentions always went sailing out of the window when I had that loaf in my hands!

I think eventually Mum accepted that was a price she had to pay if I was to get one for her! Of course, my Dad used to chuckle when he saw the bread, so I knew it would be ok! Another thing I remember about bread is that when I was at my maternal grand-mothers for tea, she would sometimes have some tinned fruit (not very often because this was a real treat). If we did have this, we always had to have some bread and butter with it. This was be-cause tinned fruit was difficult to get hold of in the war years, we couldn't have very much. For instance, if it was peaches, we would be lucky to have four slices and so had to have bread and butter to fill us up. I didn't mind too much because this Gran always cut her bread nice and thin, which was good because we couldn't have too much butter on, again because this was rationed. So all in all, tinned fruit at Grandmas even with bread and butter, was nice.

Grandma Bramley (my Mum's mum) used to bottle her own fruit, so instead of tinned fruit we would sometimes have plums. Grandma had a plum tree in her garden and some apple trees, so she would put the harvest from these to good use. When I slept at Grandma's house, the room I used had a big wardrobe in. On top of the wardrobe were always boxes of apples wrapped individu-ally in newspaper. When Grandma wanted any apples for a pie or something, she would go and get some down from the top of the wardrobe. I sometimes used to help her wrap them up. I had to be careful which apples I wrapped, because no bruises or damaged ones could be wrapped up.

Now my paternal grandmother was the opposite, her bread would be sliced like doorsteps and we would have lovely dripping on. Strange that I liked thin bread at one grandmas and thick at the other!

This grandma, Grandma Ratcliffe (my Dad's mum) didn't have any fruit trees in her garden, but my Grandad kept chickens, so when I was there I would usually be able to have a boiled egg for breakfast (again with chunky bread), which was a rare treat because eggs were also rationed.

Dripping was always a treat. My sister and I would argue about who would have the 'dig down'. This was the dark jelly like substance that would be at the bottom of the dripping and got it's name for obvious reasons! Dad sometimes used to settle the argument by saying neither of us would have it as he would! After that, Shirley and I would whisper to each other and agree who would have a turn this time. Dad would have a twinkle in his eye, and I know now he hoped we would do something like that instead of arguing. Wise Dad!

One other thing I do remember was that we always said grace before eating our meals. My Dad used to say 'May the Lord make us truly thankful for what we are about to receive', and he used to explain to us how lucky we were to have food on the table as there were many who didn't. We weren't allowed to start eating until grace had been said. We also weren't allowed to leave the table until either Mum or Dad gave us permission. Usually, they didn't make us stay there too long, but if we had gobbled things down too quickly, we were made to wait to 'let it go down'.

Ten

Sweeties and chocolate were such a treat
Not something we usually had to eat
Because of the war very few were around
And rationed they were, if any were found..............................

Being born in the early part of World War 2, I learnt not to expect sweets or chocolate very often. All sweets and chocolate bars were rationed and you weren't allowed very many for a whole month. People used to save up their points in their ration books until it was worth buying some. Even then there weren't many in the shops. Every time the shop keeper had a delivery of sweets, word would go round and people would queue up to buy some. You rarely could choose what you wanted, you had to have what was available and if you didn't get in the queue quickly enough you would be unlucky as they would have all gone and you would have to go home empty handed.

I was never allowed to go and queue but Mum or Dad would go. I remember waiting anxiously to see what they had been able to get. Then they were given out sparingly and we were told to make them last. That was a bone of contention with me, because I would make mine last, but my sister wouldn't and then would want some of mine! Because Shirley was only little, Mum would look at me and smile and say 'just let her have one'. How could I resist my lovely Mum's smile! So I would hand over one of my precious sweets, but I have to say, the thank you and smile my sister gave me, well, it was worth it.

There was one time when the word went around that the shop had some sweets come in and Dad went and joined the queue. It was a very long one and I went to see how near to the front he was. To my eyes he had a long, long wait and I thought they would be sold out when he got there. Dad sent me home and said he was sure he would get something. Eventually, Dad came home and proudly presented us with a bag of sweets. Oh how disappointed I was when I looked in the bag! They were chocolate coated nuts!! Now I loved nuts and loved chocolate but hated them together (still do). This was all they had left in the shop when it was Dad's turn. He brought them home so proudly and had queued for such a long while that, even at the young age I was, I simply couldn't let him know I didn't like them. So in true budding actress form, I made myself smile and hugged my lovely Dad, because it meant a lot to him and a lot of dad's wouldn't have queued like that for their children! Until the day he died, Dad never knew I had lied that day. I ate the sweets then, but never since!!

Because as I have said, sweets were few and far between, when we were a little older, Shirley and I used to make our own sherbet dabs! We weren't allowed to do this very often because sugar was rationed as well. We used to make two little bags in the way Mum had shown us, out of newspaper (or rather I did, and gave Shirley one), add some sugar out of the sugar bowl and some cocoa. Close the bag, give it a shake, and hey presto - a perfectly good concoction to dip your finger in and lick it off!! That would keep us happy for ages. Any dentists reading this, sorry!!

I remember my sister used to get into trouble for sticking her finger in the sugar bowl and licking it off! She never understood how Mum knew as she wasn't in the room when she did it. I had to explain (being the big sister) that Shirley had left her fingerprint in the bowl! There would be a hole in the sugar! How we laughed at that when we were grown up!

I sometimes look at the bewildering display of sweets in the shops today, and have a secret smile to myself remembering those sherbet dabs. I wonder what today's kids would make of it!

Eleven

As a child I loved to sing
Until one day a dreadful thing
Although I tried with all my might
I found that I had - STAGE FRIGHT!.....................

My mother was an accomplished pianist and singer. She would perform at local functions and sometimes at the local theatre. I discovered when I was older that Mum was booked up to go to sing to the Forces at the war front, but little old me put paid to that!! It all had to be cancelled when Mum found she was pregnant.

Music became a part of my everyday life. Mum taught the piano and there was always someone there having lessons. I used to love to sit quietly and listen to Mum teaching. Some of her pupils would be very young and Mum had a lovely way of teaching them. She would make the keys like a story book with the deep bottom notes becoming Daddy Bear and the opposite end of the scale being Baby Bear. Sometimes the keys would be angry, sometimes sad and often happy. It was no surprise that ALL of her pupils passed their exams.

Now my Dad was a different kettle of fish! He had never had a lesson in his life, but could sit at the piano and play any tune I would ask for. He liked to play jazz. So I had Mum on one hand with classical stuff and Dad on the other with 'modern' type stuff. Many a happy hour was spent with all of us, my young sister included, round the piano having a sing song. Sometimes Mum would play and sometimes Dad, and if we were lucky, they would do a duet. This was really good, because their two different styles came together and sounded great. At least to my undoubtedly biased ears!

My favourite times were when Dad and I used to harmonise. What marvellous memories I have of those times. Such a lot of fun. Because of those times, Mum discovered that I had a singing voice and encouraged me to sing. I really loved it and was really happy singing my heart out.

Mum had been involved with Music Festivals and decided it would be good for me to enter some of the competitions. So I went on the stage singing and Mum always accompanied me on the piano. I also used to enter the poetry competitions and found I was quite good at comedy poems. I would stand on the stage and recite a poem, putting actions to the words. I absolutely used to love this. However, back to what this story is really about.........one day when I was six, I was entered into a singing competition and Mum and I duly turned up ready for me to do my bit.

This was in a hall, and I have no idea where it was now. It was so long ago and it may not have registered where even at the time, except it was somewhere in Leicestershire. So we were all set, I knew my song word for word and everything seemed fine until.............oh dear me, what was that? My Mum wasn't allowed to accompany me on the piano, they had their own pianist!! We hadn't known about this beforehand and Mum was very annoyed about it, but said to me to just do exactly as if it was her at the piano. I burst into tears and wouldn't go on stage. If my mum couldn't play, I wasn't going to sing, simple as that! So other people carried on doing their acts and eventually I was persuaded to do my turn.

I got up on stage, opened my mouth but shock, horror, no words would come out of my mouth! I was in a real panic, this had never happened before. The pianist was very good and patiently hit the opening notes a couple of times and eventually, a miracle, I sang the song! The applause I got was tremendous, but I just wanted to get off the stage and go to my Mum.

Obviously, I didn't win that particular competition, but at the awards part, I got a special mention for determination and courage!! Not the outcome we wanted but some small compensation!

The first time I sang in public, I was five years old and was in my first year at school. I was picked to play the lead role of the Christmas play.

This was a lovely story about a little girl who had a dream of travelling to Bethlehem and seeing the baby Jesus. When she got there she sang Away in a Manger kneeling at the crib. Yes, that little girl was me.

The play opened with me in a bed in the centre of the stage, which had a net curtain (well that's what it looked like to me!) at the front of the stage. This was to give the dream like effect. I had to sit up and smile......oh dear, trouble already! Although I was only five, I could hold my own in an argument! My teacher said I wasn't smiling and I knew I was! Eventually, she made me realise that yes, she knew I was smiling because I was smiling with my eyes, but the audience wouldn't see that, so I had to make sure it was a big smile with my mouth!

Although I have never had any aspirations to be an actress (my sister did and fulfilled that in Canada years later), I have always been secretly quite proud of that play. After I had trekked across the desert etc following the star, when I found the stable and knelt at the baby Jesus' manger, I sang the carol with no musical accompaniment at all. It was so quiet in the audience, just me singing. It is still very vivid in my mind to this day!

My Mum studying her music

Twelve

My mouth was open, my eyes were wide
I looked at my Mum with so much pride
Her beautiful dress, a lovely blue
She'd knock 'em for six, that much I knew....................

I mentioned earlier that my Mum used to sing on stage and was well known locally for her beautiful voice. Well one really special time I remember was when my Dad took me to the theatre where Mum was singing. Oh I was so excited. I had never been allowed before. I couldn't eat my tea, I was wanting to go. Come on Dad, are you ready yet?

I had seen the dress my Mum would be wearing, hanging up in her bedroom. It had to hang on the door because it wouldn't fit in the wardrobe. I know I had heard my Mum talking to my grandma about this dress, because clothes were still being rationed.

I knew about clothes being rationed because I had to wear petticoats made from parachute silk (I hadn't a clue what that was) and sometimes there would be a printed mark on the material. I was told this was called a Utility Mark. As raw materials became scarce during the war, manufactures were encouraged by the government to be as economical with the materials as possible. Goods made to the Utility standard were marked with this stamp (picture below) and this particular material used for our petticoats was from left overs which couldn't be used for parachutes any more and therefore was sold cheaply to people to make into things. I don't know how Mum managed to get the material for this pretty dress, but I know a lady made it for her. It was a powder blue and had lots of net on top of the skirt, which was long and nearly touched the ground. It was beautiful, I had never seen anything like it.

Utility mark

We arrived at the theatre and Mum went back stage. Dad was talking to the manager of the theatre and I was hopping from one foot to the other, impatient to go inside. I had never been there before and it was so exciting. Plus I couldn't wait to see my Mum in her lovely dress, although Dad told me she wouldn't be on yet, there were other acts to go before her.

Well eventually, we went into this special place. I was told it was a box, although that didn't make any sense to me. How could seats in a theatre be called a box? Grown ups were really funny sometimes!

Finally, finally the curtains closed on the comedian who was on stage. Then the music played, the curtains opened, and there was, not my Mum, but a Fairy Queen!! I was absolutely enthralled! She looked so beautiful. Was that really my Mum? Then she began to sing. I will never, ever forget the feelings I had then. I was too young to be able to describe them properly but I did know I was so proud. I wanted to tell all those people there - Look, that's MY MUM.

When Mum had finished singing, all the people were clapping. They were clapping my Mum!! Then the curtain came down and I thought she had gone, but people were calling out and the curtain opened again and there was Mum, still there and she looked so happy. This happened another time. I didn't know what was going on but Dad told me it was called an 'encore' and they were calling for my Mum again. So she had to sing a little bit more.

I didn't know at that time, but some time in the future, I was destined to wear that beautiful dress, I tell about this later in the book.

After Mum's performance, Dad took me home and I had to go to bed. A friend of my parents was baby sitting my sister and myself as Dad went back to the theatre.

I was on cloud nine. Was any other little girl so lucky as I was. I had the best Mum and Dad in the world.

Thirteen

Some of my friends had started to learn
To ride their bikes and I did so yearn
To do the same, so went up the hill
Got on my bike and then had a spill

Cycling along, the wind in my hair
It was so good and I hadn't a care
Freedom was mine, of this I knew
As pedalling like mad, along I flew..............

I think I must have been eight years old when I got my first bike. I had wanted one for ages as some of my friends had bikes. Well the day finally arrived when my wish was granted. On my birthday, Mum and Dad proudly presented me with a bike. It wasn't new, but then during the war years and the ones immediately following, there were not many things like new bikes available. Dad had managed to get hold of one and did it up for me. It wasn't important to me if it was new or not, it was my very own bike and I loved it. Now came the learning to ride bit...........oh dear!

Dad wanted to help me to learn to ride it, but oh, no, would I listen? Of course not! Little independent me? Don't be daft! I didn't see any problem at all, it looked easy to do, you just sat on the seat, turned the pedals and away you went! Right? OK! Well if my Dad could do it, so could I!

Where we lived at the time, our house was at the bottom of a hill, the road came down, our house at the bottom and the road bent round and went on for a bit. So off I set with my bike and my friend Margaret to the top of the hill. Margaret got on her bike and sailed down the hill, no problem. I duly got on mine and followed suit! Oh yes, I sailed down the hill managing to stay on the bike, but ....bottom of the hill in sight and I either had to stop or go round the bend. Well, I hadn't thought about stopping or turning had I. Yes, straight into our hedge I went, much to Margaret's amusement and my dismay!

Mum must have been watching from the window because she came straight out to see if I was alright. Few bruises (not least to my ego!) but I was fine. Right this was not going to beat me!

Back in the saddle, I changed tactics. I rode along the pavement and used the fence along the front of next door to steady me. After practicing for about an hour (well it seemed like an hour but probably wasn't) I thought ok let's have another go at the hill. All my friends who had bikes used that hill and some of the big boys used to go really fast down it. I wanted to do it like that.

So, back up to the top of the hill I went, pushing my bike. Margaret was going to watch from the bottom. Guess what? This time I could do it! Oh the wind in my hair as I sailed down that hill, even now I can still remember the exhilaration as I flew down that hill, and the satisfaction as I mastered braking and stopping in time instead of landing in the hedge!

No stopping me now. My bike became my favourite companion for many years. When I was older and able to earn my own money, the first thing I did was to save up for a new bike. I was so proud the day I took possession of it. This was my first ever new bike and I loved it.

My love of cycling lasted until I was in my mid forties when arthritis forced me to give it up. However, I will never forget the joy I felt riding my bike. My day of learning will never be forgotten either!

Fourteen

When it was nice, we would go out
And we would be able to sing and shout
Sometimes we would go to Pignut Spinney
A name that I thought was oh so funny.............

In the nice weather, Mum, Dad, me and my sister Shirley would go out somewhere. Sometimes we would go on our bikes. Mum on hers, Dad on his, me on mine and Shirley on hers. We didn't go too far as Shirley was too young to cycle any distance and we were lucky, there were lots of picnic places quite close to us.

Dad would have a kettle on the handlebars and Mum would have tea, sugar and milk so we could have a cup of tea. If we were lucky, we might have some lemonade as well. Mum would make sandwiches and some cake to take with us and off we would go.

We often went to a spot where there was a stream and if it was a hot day, we would be able to dangle our legs in the water. Dad would always produce a ball and we would have a game, Then I would go off and have a wander. That is if I could get away without

Shirley realising because she always wanted to come with me. I didn't mind sometimes but other times I liked to day dream and you can't do that with a little sister chattering away!

Sometimes we wouldn't go out on our bikes, but just walk to somewhere locally. A popular spot was a place called Pignut Spinney. Now the very name set my imagination on fire! The first time we went, Dad explained what it meant and dug up a pig-nut to show me. It wasn't a nut at all, but reminded me of a baby parsnip!

The Pignut

Pigs used to forage or 'grub up' for them. Pignut Spinney used to lead on to the Charnwood Forest, which unfortunately is no longer there. However I have discovered that Pignut Spinney is still there although not as it was when I was a little girl. I believe it is a Nature Reserve now and there is a car park as well. Who would have dreamed of that happening when I was little!

It was a marshy place when we used to go all those years ago. Sometimes the farmer who farmed nearby used to put his cows in there and let them roam, with the resulting outcome that we had to beware of cowpats when we walked through there!

Ha ha! Try to tell my little exuberant sister to watch where she was walking! Shirley didn't walk anywhere, it was a full pace run! Needless to say, I lost count the number of times Mum had to do a clean up job on her! Shirley would wriggle and didn't want to stay still while Mum got her sorted.

We didn't have cups of tea or a picnic when we went there. It was just a chance to be in the fresh air and as the stream went through the spinney there was always something to see in there. We only went there if the cows had been moved because my Mum was nervous of them, so Dad would check first before we went.

It was usually a tired little group that wended their way home after one of these walks. Shirley and I were always really hungry when we got back. Two tired little girls would go to bed that night and go 'out like a light' as Mum would say.

Doesn't sound much does it, out for a walk with Mum and Dad, but somehow whatever we did with our parents, it always evolved into fun.

Fifteen

My Mum she would the organ play
When in church on each Sunday
And when I was bored, I used to puff
And blow the little bits of fluff

What's that all about, you ask with surprise
If you read below, I will put you wise............

In my early years, we would go to church every Sunday and Mum would play the organ. I had been allowed to see the organ and where Mum sat to play it. I was absolutely fascinated! You had to pull out button things which I was told were called organ stops. This seemed daft to me, because they didn't stop the organ playing!

We had a piano at home and this was so different. Grown ups did have a fascinating world, it all seemed so exciting.

I wanted to stay and watch Mum play the organ for the hymns but wasn't allowed. Oh no! I had to go and sit with Dad, Grandma and Grandad and my sister on the seats that weren't called seats at all, but were called pews. Grown ups never failed to amaze me, why was a seat called a pew and not a seat? This growing up business can be so difficult to understand!

Anyway, this is where it stopped being interesting anymore because we had to sit quietly and listen to the minister talking. Now, I didn't understand what he was saying and so stopped listening. Oh dear, boredom was setting in. What to do to pass the time until we could sing a hymn and I could hear Mum play the organ?

My Grandma Bramley used to like knitting and did it a lot. She would make a lot of things and would make things for Shirley and me like jumpers and cardigans. Sometimes gloves and scarves, even little dolls. I thought she was very clever. She actually taught me to knit and sew. I once embroidered a set of mats for Grandma's dressing table and I was so touched after she had died to discover she had kept it all those years.

One of the things Grandma knitted for us, was something called a bolero (another fascinating word). This was a bit like a cardigan but without sleeves and didn't button up at the front.

Our boleros would be all fluffy and I was told they were made from a wool called angora, which came from the Angora rabbit. These would be so fluffy and it didn't take Shirley and me long to discover that you could gently pull bits of fluff off!

We would wear these boleros to church sometimes and it became a favourite pastime of ours when we were sitting really bored in church, to sit and pull bits of fluff off and gently blow it. Low and behold, it would float over peoples heads and they didn't even notice! They would sit there listening to the preacher and a bit of fluff would waft by their faces. We used to see if we could blow hard enough to make it float to the ceiling! Then we would get the giggles and it would be discovered by Grandma what we had been up to.

Of course as I was the oldest, I was the one in trouble. I was told I was 'setting a bad example' to Shirley! Oh dear! Who would ever imagine a bit of fluff would cause trouble!

Eventually, Mum got to hear about it and we weren't allowed to wear our lovely fluffy boleros to church anymore. Oh well, I guess all good things come to an end! I can't remember what I did after that to stop being bored in church. Perhaps I started to listen properly to the preacher??

So, I learnt that church was good for listening to Mum playing the organ, singing hymns (which I loved doing) and watching fluff float! What an education!

Sixteen

I loved all of my grandparents you see
But they were as different as they could be
One house was quiet and peaceful and calm
The other you felt was in for a storm

Oh baby chicks would I see you
Hatch from your shells, I wanted to
Would I be awake in time to see
You hatching out just there for me...................

Because both of my parents were at work, when it came to school holidays, Shirley and I would go to one of the grandparents houses. Shirley would go to one and me the other. Then on the next holiday, we would swap and go to the other one.

My two sets of grandparents were very different in many ways. Grandma and Grandad Bramley's home was a quiet and peaceful place. It always looked light, airy and calm. I loved being there.

Now my Grandma and Grandad Ratcliffe's home was as unlike my other grandparents home as was possible.

This home made you feel something exciting could happen. It was always full of people and far from being quiet and peaceful, it was a vibrant place. Noisy with lots of laughter.

My Grandad Ratcliffe had been poorly and I knew later he had tuberculosis (he was to die when I was about nine). He had to give up his job in the shoe factory at the end of the road, and worked as a night watchman. I loved it when he did this as I used to sneak through a gap in the fence surrounding the place where he worked, and go to sit with him and his mates around the glowing brazier. I really loved going to see him and doing this. All of his mates would make a fuss of me, which of course, I loved.

Grandad would let me stay for a while and then send me back home to be with Grandma. As he explained, he would get into trouble if his boss saw me there.

I loved Grandad very much and used to sit on his knee in his special chair. This was a wooden chair with a high back and arms. Grandma had made a cushion for the seat and another that went up the back. Nobody but Grandad sat in this chair. (My Dad had it for many years later on, after Grandad had died).

I can remember so clearly, sitting at the dinner table when I was there, and being given something to eat that I didn't like very much and didn't want to eat. Grandad would look at me and say 'come on lassie, get it down your mussy' and guess what? I did.

Because Grandad wasn't allowed to do a full time job, money was scarce. Well it always seemed to be anyway with everyone, but now it was worse for them. So Grandad took up shoe repairing as well as the night watchman job. There was a cellar which you got to through a door in the sitting room. This is where Grandad did his shoe repairs for people. It seemed quite scary to me. Although Grandad had a light in there, it still seemed dark and gloomy to me. Nevertheless, I would spend as much time as I could down there, watching Grandad at work.

Grandad also kept chickens in his garden. A lot of people did this to help with the rations at the time. I can't remember how many eggs were allowed to each person, although I do remember sharing half an egg sometimes with my Dad. We also had big tins of dried eggs which Mum and Grandma made cakes with. This puzzled me for a long while, how could an egg which was a runny thing when it was broken open, turn into this yellow powder stuff?

Once when I was staying at this Grandad's house, he told me there was going to be some chickens hatch out very soon. Might even be tomorrow morning. I desperately wanted to see them hatch out and pleaded to be allowed up early to see them. Grandad said yes if I was awake I could come down and see them.

Well when I stayed there I had to sleep in the middle of the big bed my two aunties slept in. I didn't mind, I was always asleep when they came to bed, and they were nice. They both had boyfriends and would tell me about going out to the pictures and on their bikes with them.

On this particular occasion I went to bed and was so excited it took me a while to go to sleep. Anyway, I slept and woke up to daylight. I didn't know what time it was, but knew I should get up if I wanted to see the chickens hatch. So I tried to get out of the bed and it meant climbing over one of my aunties. Oh dear, now I had a problem! First Auntie Marjory woke up and said it was too early, I should go back to sleep, then after a little while, I tried again, this time over the other auntie, Auntie Lillian. Of course, she woke up as well and again I was told to go back to sleep. I tried to explain about the chickens but to no avail.

You all know what happened next don't you? Naturally. I fell asleep and when I woke the next time I was allowed to get up and of course, I was too late! However, I forgot to be cross and sulk (not that I ever sulked, but my cousin did) because the little chicks were so lovely.

My cousin Diane would sulk and Grandma would make her go and stand in the corner. I used to think how stupid it was to sulk, Diane knew she would get sent to the corner, but still sulked.

I have to say, I still loved both my aunties in spite of this. They were really nice to me and would let me help them when they were getting ready to go out with their boyfriends. I loved to watch them put make up on, especially lipstick.

Auntie Marjory had a lovely boyfriend who was in the army. When he was home on leave, Uncle Ron as I called him, used to ride a motorbike and Auntie Marjory would ride on the back. I thought this was so exciting.

One day Auntie Marjory and Uncle Ron were at home looking after me while Grandma was out somewhere with Grandad. They decided we would make some chips. I had never had chips at home before, only from the chip shop. I don't even know if there were such things as deep fat fryers then. I doubt it. Anyway, Uncle Ron did these chips and he cut the potatoes up like real chips from the chippy. Then he cooked them in the frying pan. It took quite a while to do them as he could only do a few at a time. These were the best chips I have ever tasted.

It really wasn't so bad being a little girl after all!

Eventually, Auntie Marjorie married her army boyfriend and he became my Uncle Ron for real then. They had a long and happy marriage, unfortunately they are no longer here but they left me with happy memories.

Unfortunately, in the intervening years, my lovely grandad died. I was so sad, he was a really lovely man. I was very upset with my parents for a long while afterwards, because I wasn't allowed to go to the funeral. It was deemed I was too young and would find it too upsetting. This was one of the very few times I really disagreed with my parents, but I did as I was told and went to school while my darling grandad was buried.

Maybe they were right, I did accept that eventually, but for a long while I felt hurt and shut out. I know that wasn't Mum and

Dad's intention and because, although young, I knew in my heart they were thinking of me and I never spoke of it afterwards. I said a prayer for him when I went to bed. We were brought up to always say out prayers before bed each night and grandad was in mine for a very long while.

Seventeen

My Grandma Bramley loved me a lot
When out with her I always got
A special treat for all to see
A big meringue was just for me

My Grandad Bramley was nice as well
He had a glass eye, I know, I could tell
He put it in a box at night
Poor Grandad, it wasn't right

Glass eye and meringues, what do I mean?
I'll tell you more, it will be seen……………

Life in my other grandparents, Grandad and Grandma Bramley's house was different as can be from my paternal grandparents.

My Mum had been left in a children's home when she was very young and was adopted by Grandad and Grandma Bramley when she was seven. They lived a lifestyle so unlike my Dad's parents, where life always seemed so hectic.

Everything was calm and orderly at this grandparents house. Both of them were members of the local Methodist church and a lot of their activities revolved around church.

When I stayed with them, they would take me to most of these activities, which I didn't mind because everyone would make a fuss of me.

Grandma used to go to some kind of gatherings sometimes, (I don't know what the purpose of these were, I don't think I was ever told) and very often we would sit at long benches in a church room, and there would be cakes at various intervals along these benches. I believe there would be about six or seven of these benches, so that was quite a lot of plates of cakes!

These cakes would be a mixture of all kinds including maybe a meringue. This was at a time just after the war had ended and it was amazing to see such cakes. Of course, ingredients and suchlike were becoming more readily available and people were indulging themselves just a little.

As I was born at the beginning of the war, I had grown up so far with no knowledge whatsoever of lots of lovely treats. Meringues were one of them! After I had tasted my very first meringue, I was hooked! I could have eaten them all day and nothing else. Wow, I thought they were marvellous.

Of course, my Grandma knew this, and (much to my embarrassment), when we went to one of these teas, Grandma would say to all on our bench, 'Oh do you think you could pass that meringue for my grandaughter, she loves them'. Oh dear, although I thought it was amazing that she would do this for me, at the same time I wanted the floor to open a hole up and let me crawl into it!!

Those kind ladies, not only passed down their meringue for me, ladies on other tables started to send me theirs as well! A very fond memory and I still love meringues.

My Grandad Bramley was a very kind and jolly man. I understood he had had a hard life in his upbringing as I heard his parents were very poor and he had to work very hard. He wouldn't talk about his early life to me at all. I was naturally curious, but he wouldn't tell me anything.

I never found out exactly how he lost his eye either. I was only told he had been involved in an accident with a mine. Whether this was in the first war or a coal mine accident I never knew. All I knew was he only had one eye and had to put a glass one in the other eye socket each morning and take it out at night.

Well, you can understand the fascination to a young child. Grandad took his eye out every evening and put it in a box and his teeth out and put them in a glass!! I thought that so amazing!

These grandparents had a large horsewhip hanging on the wall in their kitchen. Now again, I have no idea why, nobody would tell me. I only know that my sister and I would be threatened with it if we were naughty! I have to say, I don't think it was ever taken off the wall, except for cleaning, but that was another fascinating thing about visiting there.

My sister used to scare me a little because we would be allowed out to play in the road when we visited these grandparents. There would be lots of us children playing in the road (we rarely saw a car down there, horses and carts were still in use quite a lot). We would play skipping games or hopscotch and were always oblivious to time. As Shirley was five years younger than me, she had to go in for bedtime half an hour earlier than me. She bitterly resented this.

Grandma would come out and call Shirley in for bed and she would kick up a fuss because I was allowed to stay out longer. I used to offer to go in as well, but Grandma wouldn't hear of it. She would say, Shirley has to learn she can't have her own way! Oh dear, this upset me as I didn't like to see my little sister cry and I used to say to her 'go in or they might get the whip down'. I thought this would frighten her and make her go in but oh, no, not my sister. That only made her more determined to argue! We have had many a laugh since about those times.

Oh and by the way, Grandma always won even though she never lifted a finger and the whip stayed on the wall!!

One thing I always enjoyed when staying with these Grandparents was going out on long walks with them. Shirley didn't come with us as she was too young and we walked a long way. We would catch a bus to take us out into the country and then walk back home through fields and country lanes.

They would pick different routes and although I was so very tired when we got back home, I loved it all. We would have sandwiches and a flask of tea to keep us going until we got home at teatime. Not a proper picnic like we had with Mum and Dad, and we didn't have fun and games, but good nevertheless. If we were lucky, we might see a fox or other animals, and lots of wild flowers.

One thing that used to puzzle me when we were out like this. My grandparents were very religious and strong believers in law and order, but on these walks they became different people! If we walked through a farmer's field of cabbages, they would have to take a cabbage! Never anything else and I know they didn't ever do anything like that normally. I don't know if maybe it started in the war when everything was scarce, seems the most likely thing. Grandma would say the farmer wouldn't miss just this one! It was another side to my God-fearing grandparents!

Although until I was older, the war didn't really mean much to me except for the planes going over and when you could hear bombs going off, it did come home to me just how bad it was when my Grandma Bramley took me to Nottingham. She wanted to go and see some relatives who lived there. These people lived in a flat, which I thought was great. I had never seen a flat before.

This was just after war had ended and all major cities had a lot of buildings and houses reduced to rubble. These relatives were not particular close, I had to call the lady Auntie and think she was a cousin of my Grandma's. She had three sons who were nearly grownup, at least at five years old, that's what I thought. I didn't see them for very long as they were all getting ready to go out somewhere.

On our way there, we saw so much devastation it was dreadful. I hadn't seen anything like this before as living in Loughborough, we escaped most of the bombing. Leicester got a lot but I didn't go there when I was little. Probably too dangerous to take me, although I know Mum and Dad went sometimes. Mum used to want to buy sheet music for playing the piano and could often only get what she wanted in Leicester.

After we arrived in Nottingham, the grown ups started to talk about the war. One of the brothers said, "Look, this is how close we came to disaster", and went to the back door, opened it and when we looked out, it was a sheer drop!!

The flats in the building next door had caught a bomb and there was just rubble on the ground. When I looked out across the horizon, I could see what horror it must have been. So much was just rubble. We hadn't seen all of this on our way there. It is a sight that, although I was very young, has never left. It is imprinted in my memory for ever. I think that was the moment that I realised just exactly what had been going on.

I had been very fortunate to have been shielded from such devastation, living just that bit away from a city.

Grandad and Grandma Bramley

Eighteen

Oh to see them up there in the tree
All round and shining as can be
I'd climb up the tree we'd found
And throw the apples to the ground

Then all of a sudden my friends would flee
Leaving me up there, oh dearie me…………………

A favourite pastime of us all when I was growing up, was of course, scrumping. We would set off, my friends and I, to find a tree with lots of apples on them, all ready for eating.

We knew where the most popular trees were, but that wasn't the only thing to take into consideration. We would also check whether the owner of the tree we were thinking of was at home or not. Now this wasn't always easy to tell in those days when normal, ordinary folk didn't have cars. Of course, rich people sometimes had a car, but they didn't always use them when they went out, I now know because petrol was scarce in those days.

Naturally, our judgement of the situation was frequently wrong, and many a time I would belt along the country lanes back home like a thing possessed! It was no wonder I was a skinny little thing when I think of all the times I would run like the wind.

Of course, sometimes we didn't get away in time, and then that meant trouble. Our parents would be told and occasionally, the headmaster or headmistress at school would be informed! Oh dear that was disaster. That could mean double trouble! I remember a time one of my friends, a little boy called John, was smacked by his mum for scrumping and then when he got to school, he was caned by his teacher as well! I was very lucky that never happened to me.

There was one time though when I was caught actually up the tree. Because I was probably the most agile in our little group (or possibly the most stupid), I almost always was the one who climbed up the tree, picked the apples and threw them down to my friends, who would gather them up and we would have a share out later.

Normally I would keep an eye open for anyone coming and so would my friends on the ground, but this time we were caught unawares. In spite of my good intentions, it wasn't easy keeping an eye on the path while trying to pick apples to throw down, at the same time as keeping from falling off the tree! Nobody heard the man coming up and the first I knew was all my friends scattering and running off. Well what was I to do, stuck up a tree, apples in my hands ready to throw down? Well all I could think of was letting the apples go, climbing down and looking as meek and mild as I know how. You have never seen a better actress, believe me! The very best sorrowful, forlorn, don't tell me off mister please, look I could manage! I probably looked scared to death!

Fortunately for me, this was a very nice kind man, who maybe remembered doing the same thing when he was a boy. All he did was tell me never to do it again and he didn't ever want to see me up his tree, and he let me go.

This time I think I must have broken records getting home. I do remember being extra good for a while to try and make up and because I was so grateful for getting off so lightly.

However, this wasn't the only thing I did in that line. There were allotments next door to our house! Now if ever that was an invitation to be naughty, I don't know what was! I would get behind my Dad's runner beans where I knew Mum couldn't see me from the window and dig a hole under the fence big enough for me to crawl under (I did say I was tiny didn't I?). Carrots, raspberries, peas all went the same way. These were for eating on the spot. I would then crawl back again and cover up the hole I had made.

My Dad must have wondered about the disturbed earth when he was gardening, but nothing was ever said, so I presume I got away with it!

I never ever went hungry in those days, even though food was rationed and lots of things were scarce, so I really had no reason for scrumping the apples and pinching things to eat from the allotment. I conclude it was the excitement of doing something I knew was wrong. I really must add that it was only one carrot or a couple of raspberries or peas. I would have been surprised if the allotment holders ever knew, except probably scratching their heads at the earth around the carrots looking different!

Everybody grew vegetables in their gardens then and some even had an allotment as well, because of the scarcity of food in the shops. The government of the day were always encouraging people to do this (there was a slogan they used: 'Dig for Victory', and even people with a very tiny garden would grow something. Quite a lot of people would have their own chickens as well so they would be able to have eggs.

I remember my Mum putting cream from the top of the milk into a muslin bag and hanging it from a tree in the garden, to make cottage cheese.

Some of the things people made during those days to make food more interesting was amazing. It was surprising how many imaginations worked overtime when people thought up something new to make with the limited supplies available.

Cakes were made without eggs or sometimes dried eggs which was like a funny yellowy colour, and substitutions were used for so many things. Coffee was a rare commodity too, usually it was chicory in a bottle. The expression 'make do and mend' was also very commonplace.

I often think if we had continued in this way over the years, there would have been no need of recycling bins etc now as that's what we did as a matter of course.

Nineteen

The grocers shop was a fascinating place
The grocer would have a smile on his face
He would cut up the butter and shape with a pat
It went in our dish to take home like that

We would take our own bags to put things in
And he would cut our bacon so nice and thin
He'd weigh up the sugar and also the tea
It wasn't in packets like now, you see....................

I used to think the grocers shop was a marvellous place and while waiting our turn in the queue to be served, I would watch the grocer serving people in front.

If customers wanted some tea, he would use a scoop to get the tea leaves out of a big sack and then weigh them on the big scales. Finally putting them into the tin the customer had brought with them.

I liked it best when someone wanted butter. It was so fascinating watching him cut a lump of butter from a big block, and then using two wooden things that looked like paddles, but which were called butter pats, he would make the butter into shapes. When he had the right shape, he would get a wooden stamp, and make a mark on the butter to show which farmer had made the butter.

I would have loved to have done that, and for a very short period wanted to be a grocer when I grew up!!

I can remember my Grandma Bramley would sometimes buy some butter that would be shaped into a round. I thought that was great, but she wouldn't buy it very often because apparently, it was the 'best' butter and cost more money.

We always took our own bags with us to put things in, Sometimes we would even make our own and I used to make them for Mum using milk bottle tops. Not everyone had milk delivered in bottles although my Mum did, but when I went to Grandma Ratcliffe's to stay, the milkman would come round with his horse and cart and the milk would be in big containers. You would take your own jug or dish outside to him in the road and he would fill it up for you.

The milkman who delivered to our house, had his milk in bottles with a cardboard top that had a bit cut out you had to push in to lift the top off. We would save these cardboard tops, cover them with wool or string, join them together to make a bag or something similar. Now there was recycling at it's best!!

There were lots of people walking around with different coloured home made bags in those days.

I don't remember Mum or either of my Grandmother's going to buy vegetables at the greengrocers when I was very small, because we always grew our own. I don't think there was very much choice in them at that time anyway. I know people would think they had a prize if they bought an onion!

It was always good if you were able to buy some sweets, because these were usually in great big jars and would be in rows on a shelf at the back of the counter. I would look at them while waiting to be served and wonder if I would be able to have certain ones or would they cost too much money.

Sweets weren't always available at the time I was growing up because of rationing, but as soon as they were off ration and available again, that was how it was.

During the period of rationing, if you were lucky, the shopkeeper would have one jar with sweets in, and sometimes it would be empty.

When you had chosen which sweeties you wanted, the shopkeeper would weigh them out on his big scales, and you would watch to see how many you would get. Sometimes, but not very often, an extra one would slip in and the shopkeeper would leave it. That was the best of luck and you would excitedly tell your friends!!

Another memory of this time, was going with my dad to the local market. This would always be on a Saturday morning, and I think Dad and I would go so Mum could catch up on housework without us around.

We would look at all the different stalls but there was one we always went to before coming home. It was a meat stall which sold, among lots of meat and other things, potted meat. This was my Mum's favourite and I grew to love it as well. We would look for the little square boxes with a white top, which was the fat from the meat, underneath would be the lovely potted meat. I have never tasted any so good. The stuff you buy in little jars today is absolutely no comparison to that delicious spread from the market. It was considered a special treat, because it was a bit more expensive than some others you could buy.

Twenty

Are you sitting comfortably? Then we'll start the play
Pretending to be film stars, acting and singing away
But beware on the streets that you don't slide
On those sheets of glass we made with such pride..................

We had many ways of amusing ourselves when I was growing up, hopscotch, skipping, skimming cigarette cards and many, many others.

We devised all kinds of things to do indoors as well as playing outside, one of which I used to love doing was French knitting. An empty cotton reel was needed for this (they were all made from wood in those days which was ideal), along with four tacks from your dad's tool box. Dad would hammer the four tacks into one end of the cotton reel and all you needed then was wool. Mums and grandmothers always had spare wool for this. Oh I nearly forgot, you would also need a crochet hook to pull the wool over the tacks. I believe this is still being used nowadays by young girls, although I think they are probably bought all ready made from the shops these days.

French knitting

As you 'knitted' the wool formed a cord like a snake and you pulled this through the hole in the cotton reel. When it was long enough you coiled it round and stitched it together. This would then turn into a dressing table mat, or a cover for the dolls pram, or anything your imagination would run to. It would grow very quickly at first, then seemed to take ages to grow long enough to do much with. Oh dear, I think I must have been quite an impatient little girl!

Another things girls would do was to make their hair grips pretty. We all wore hair grips in our hair then and they were very plain and boring (still are I think). So we would buy some plastic coated electrical wire from the ironmongers. The wire we bought came in different colours and was quite thin. We would then put it around the hair grip using a blanket stitch, only putting it on the one side which would be on top and could be seen by others when the grip was in your hair. Woe betide any girl who didn't have one! I remember our local ironmonger frequently running out of this particular kind of wire! Until, that is, we got bored with doing that and found something else to start a new fashion with. Fashion conscious little girls even in the bleak days during and following the war!

Mostly though, we preferred to be outside playing. When winter time came, that was lots of fun. There were sledges to make, slides to perfect until they were a sheet of glass, and if we were really lucky, snowmen to make and snowballs to throw.

I never made a sledge for myself, because I had a friend called David who would let me share his. David lived two doors away from me and we played together quite a lot.

Later on when we had moved house and lived in Oxford, I would go with the friends I made there to the local golf course when it had snowed. With the slopes it made a terrific place to use our sledges on. I can remember being so cold my fingers were numb, but it was so much fun and really exhilarating that I would just keep on going. But that was when I was a bit older, in the meantime we were still living in Loughborough in Leicestershire.

The thing I also loved doing when we had snow and ice, was making a slide. When I think back now, how dangerous to people walking along the pavements this was, especially to older people.

We would start it off by rubbing our feet along the ground in the snow and ice until you could slide a bit, then just making it a bit longer until it was a decent length to slide along. After that, the more you slid, the shinier and glassier it got until you could see your face in it.

Then we would take turns having a slide. You would take a good run before you got to it, then hurl yourself along the icy path. It was fantastic! The more you used it, the better it got.

Heaven knows what would happen if children still did this now. I can see the headlines in the national dailies 'little girl arrested for making dangerous slide'!! Seriously though, it really is a good job this doesn't happen nowadays (or maybe it does somewhere?).

A much safer pastime was collecting cigarette cards to use for skimming along a flat surface with a wall behind. In those days, cigarette packets had cards in them, much like the type of thing available in cereal packets today. They would be of sportsman, nature, film stars and indeed, anything. Although obviously, us children didn't go round buying packets of cigarettes, we all knew loads of grown ups who did. I think just about everyone smoked in those days. So it was quite easy to collect the cards, you just got round any grown up you knew to save them for you.

The aim of the game was to cover a card with the one you skimmed, then you would win that card. We were all trying to save whole sets of these cards and many swaps went on. The poor smokers of the day were constantly being pestered by children for their cigarette cards.

Something else my sister and our friends tried our hands at, was making perfume! We would collect as many rose petals as possible, put them in a bucket and cover them all with water. After about a day, if we could wait that long, we would use an old piece of muslin, which was used quite a lot then to cover milk etc, to then strain the rose petals through. The remaining water was supposed to be perfume!!

There were many, many ways we would find to amuse ourselves. When I think back, we were quite ingenious with all the different ideas we would come up with. Putting on a show for your parents and relatives was another way of passing the time.

We would make a 'stage' with old boxes and material Mum gave us and dress up in old clothes to put on a play. All the relatives would sit in chairs we placed in rows and patiently watch. We would also sing songs. What parents had to put up with!

I can honestly say, I don't remember ever being bored in the whole of my growing up years. There was always something to do or see or investigate. Of course we did seem to have so much more freedom then. When grown-ups had been so concerned with the possibility of being blown up by a bomb, I think the mad antics of children paled into insignificance.

Oh yes, that reminds me of something else we did. Playing in the bomb shelters. As I was only five years old when the war ended, I only have dim recollections of actual wartime events that made it all seem real. I do remember sometimes going down the bomb shelter when the air raid siren went. Even at a young age, the sound of the siren going off made me scared and would make me shiver. I hated going down the shelters, there were so many people and it was really stuffy.

A lot of times, we would go into the cupboard under the stairs. This was much better as Mum had put a sort of bed in there for me and I wasn't so scared as I was in the air raid shelter. However, the shelters made good places to play in or at least, so thought a lot of children. I didn't, they were always scary places to me but I had to show face and didn't let on about my fears but joined in when the others wanted to play in them. So many a game revolved round hiding there.

There was one other game we used to play that I hated. That was Kiss-chase. This was always played at school at break times as there was a big field with some trees around it that we used to play in.

It always seemed to be a boy who would suggest playing this! It's a wonder I wasn't picked to run for England the way I would run when playing that. Many a cut I would get when I tripped over in my haste to get away. I was so scared of being caught and kissed! Strangely enough, that fear didn't last past my teenage years!! Hmm!

Twenty One

One day at school was quite sad
To me it was so very bad
I learnt I had a lazy eye
It made me feel that I would cry

Wearing glasses would be the worst
In my class I was the very first.........................

One day, when I was seven, all of my class were told we were going to have a medical. Now this conjured up all kinds of things in my mind. I mean, what was a medical? I had a very active imagination!

When I got home and gave Mum the note that said she had to go as well, I asked her what a medical was. What did it mean? Mum then explained that a doctor would check that I was healthy and fit and nothing was wrong with me. I told Mum, why would he want to do that, of course I was healthy and nothing was wrong with me. I knew that!

Anyway, the day came and Mum turned up. Everything was fine, the doctor said I was healthy and had nothing wrong with me. I glanced across at my Mum and gave a look that said 'I told you so' , at least that is what Mum told me later.

The last thing to be checked was my eyesight and I didn't see any problems there. After all, I read lots of things and the newspaper (the cartoon strips anyway) every day, so there couldn't be anything wrong with my eyesight could there? Wrong!

I couldn't read all the letters on the board when one eye was covered up. I could when the other eye was covered but not this one. Mum said to me, 'Oh come on Ann, you can read that' and the optician looked at Mum and said 'No Mrs Ratcliffe, she can't'. Oh dear, disaster. Mum gave me a hug and said she was sorry for being cross, she really had no idea there was anything wrong.

This was not a very happy time for me as I was scared of what would happen. I didn't know of anyone who wore glasses then and felt I would be a freak. Well before I had any glasses, I had to have checks on my eyes. The thing I hated and really did scare me was when they put drops in my eyes and it made everything go blurry for a whole day! Mum assured me the effects would wear off and it would all be ok, but I wasn't convinced. I couldn't read the comic strip in the paper and I always had a bit of fun with Dad about that. I think that upset me more than anything.

Anyway, as Mum had said the effects did wear off and I could see ok again. Phew!! Then the day came when I had my glasses. Now in those days there was only one type of glasses children could have unless you had a lot of money to pay for them, so I had brown round horrible glasses. I really hated them and to make matters worse, I had to wear a patch over one eye for an hour every day as well. Fortunately, I could do this when I went home from school for dinner so nobody at school saw me.

There was something that really hurt. The first day I went to school wearing my glasses, my best friend wouldn't sit next to me and didn't even talk to me! Then some horrible boys called me four eyes! Now I had been a popular little girl up until then, how could things change so quickly! I found it hard to understand and cried in my Dad's arms that night.

Dad was wonderful and explained that it wasn't that my friends didn't like me any more, but it was something different for them to understand. He put things in such a lovely way that before we had finished talking, I was actually beginning to feel a little sorry for my friends.

An important thing Dad taught me that night, was how to laugh at myself. He said that if I showed I was happy about my glasses and could laugh when someone said 'four eyes' and answer back something like 'well at least I have got more to see with than you have', then there would be no point in taking the mickey out of me. The whole point of taking the mickey was to make the other person embarrassed or upset, and if that wasn't happening there would be no point in doing it. Do you know what? He was right. I did as he said and my best friend was still my best friend and the boys never, ever, called me four eyes again.

Thankfully, a couple of years later Mum and Dad were able to buy me some better glasses. Still National Health, but much better. These were a sort of clear pink and I felt much better about them.

There was a really funny side to all this of me wearing glasses, my little sister pretended she couldn't see properly so she could have glasses like me! Little did she know it would take the next fifty years to go by before that wish came true!

Everything really does have a funny side you know!

Twenty Two

Distemper orange, distemper green
'Twas a wall like you had never seen
Oh so cheerful and bright
To all who come into it's sight.........................

When I was quite young, I remember my Dad put a notice up on our wall in the kitchen. It read 'be careful where you go Daddy, because Ann is coming too' . I used to think that was so funny and giggled every time I saw it. Teach by example was Dad's way. One thing I most definitely learnt by following my parents example was how to enjoy life. There were many occasions when money was really scarce, but there was always fun at home.

I recall one time Dad decided to decorate the sitting room. Well there was no money for paper and people used to use distemper a lot then, so Dad bought some orange distemper and painted the sitting room walls. Fine, that looked ok to me, but it wasn't enough for Dad. He then got some green distemper and dotted the orange walls all over with green blobs! He said it was called stippling. I thought it looked funny but Mum and Dad both liked it, and when Dad was doing it, they both laughed so much.

The three of us remembered this in later years (Shirley was only a baby then) and had such a chuckle over it. Dad said you always had to make the best of things.

At least it was cheerful and anybody who came to visit always smiled when they saw it, so I suppose it must have been alright! I wonder now what the people who moved in when we left that house, thought of it!

Dad and I used to share a secret too! Dad liked to play music on the radio quite loud and Mum would call out from the other room "Harold, please turn that down, it is too loud". Dad would go to the radio, look at me and wink, pretend to touch the knob and then say "Is that better dear?". Mum would always say "Yes, thank you". I still don't know if she knew or not.

We had a big dining table then which had leaves that folded back, so part of the underneath was on top if you wanted to make it bigger. Dad made that into a games board. He marked out shove ha'penny on it and we used to play that. He also devised games I can no longer remember. We had a lot of fun with that table. Mum and Dad used to have friendly arguments when it was meal time and we were playing on the table, because Mum would want to set the table for our meal and Dad wouldn't want to pack up the game yet. There were always board games and cards played at home. Many a happy hour was spent playing something together, and if any friends came round they would always join in.

My Mum and Dad used to love playing dominoes together and I learnt to play when I was quite young. They enjoyed dominoes right through their lives and sometimes used to go to bed early with a cup of cocoa each and the pegboard and dominoes on the bed between them.

So many things were 'do it yourself' in those days, from making your own games to making your own medicine. When my sister or myself had a cough, Mum would make a concoction of brown sugar, honey, butter and vinegar. I actually quite liked this and always wanted more than Mum gave me. It always seemed to work and our coughs would get better.

The other thing I liked but which wasn't a home made thing, was the cod liver oil and malt that I had to have a spoonful of every morning before going to school. The government of the day decreed it should be available free for children. All children were given this and most didn't like it but I liked the malty taste. I wasn't so keen on the orange juice we were given though. It wasn't sweet and had a funny taste, but you learnt not to argue about things like that, because you knew it was best for you to take as with so many fruits and foods being scarce, it was a way of helping children stay healthy.

The only time I can remember being fed up because things were rationed was when Mum got me some new boots for the winter time. They were good warm boots, but they were brown! Now for some reason I can't remember, I did not want brown. I thought they were horrible. Mum said that was all she could get and if I didn't wear them I would get cold feet and might be ill, and if I was she wouldn't look after me. While I secretly didn't believe that, a little part of me was a bit scared to try it out just in case, so brown boots went on my feet every morning during those cold snowy mornings.

I was pretty glad I had nice warm feet when I used to call for my friend on the way to school. When it was a frosty morning we would get a twig from a tree and bend it to form a loop, then collect spiders webs in it. The more you could get the better, you just kept adding a layer, but you had to avoid the spider. We called them magic looking glasses. They were so pretty with the frost on them and when you held them up to the light they would shine in different colours. I don't know how many times we were late for school because we were collecting spiders webs. It didn't seem to matter how cold we got. Well not until we got to school anyway and realised we could hardly feel our fingers.

These were days when we would all huddle round the fire when we got home from school. There were no other rooms heated and when it was bedtime we would get undressed in front of the fire and race upstairs to get into bed. Mum would always put a lovely warm hot water bottle in our beds for us. I would put my head right under the bedclothes so my nose didn't get cold.

Then would come the morning and there would be icicles on the window on the inside as well as the outside! I would count to three and then jump out of bed and run downstairs where I knew it would be warm, because Mum would have been up early and lit the fire. So it was a case of getting dressed by the fire and having a lovely hot cup of cocoa. Then breakfast and off to school.

Everyone at school always used to try to sit near the radiators to keep warm, but they weren't really very warm anyway. Our teachers used to make us go outside and do exercises to get us all warmed up. And although we always grumbled about this, I have to say they did work. We would go back into our classes with our cheeks glowing and yes, we would be warm.

No matter what the weather, we always had to go out to play at break times. I don't think anyone really minded because there were so many games we would play and so much to chat to your friends about.

One thing my school friends and I always looked forward to was the Loughborough Street Fair. This fair has been held in Loughborough since an official charter was granted to the Lord of the Manor in 1221 by King Henry III.

It is held over three days and is still there every year in November now. The whole of the centre of Loughborough was closed (still is) from Thursday through to Saturday at 12 midnight.

This is the most spectacular fair, I believe in the country, with travelling showman from all parts of the country attending. Us school children would be given free tickets to go on some of the rides. This is one fair that the whole community was so proud of. Wonderful memories of that great fair.

Twenty Three

A doctor or a herbalist? Which one would you choose
My Grandma liked the herbalist she would often use
But these were few and far between, to visit them was rare
So doctors you would have to see, they always gave good care................

My Grandma Bramley didn't have a lot of faith in doctors and was very interested in herbal remedies for illnesses. In those day, there were a few herbalists around the country but not very many. They were still an unknown quantity and some were still regarded as nothing more than modern day witches. Where we lived in Loughborough, there wasn't one at all. The nearest one to us was in Leicester.

I remember visiting there with my Grandma when she wanted a herbal remedy for something (I'm afraid I cannot remember what), and was amazed at the place. We had to go upstairs to a waiting room and sat there for what seemed to me to be a very long while, then we went into the herbalists room. This was so fascinating! Bottles and jars all around the room and pills in big boxes. It was so different to our doctors surgery.

Grandma talked to the herbalist and she bought some ointment from him, and we travelled back home to Loughborough on the bus. This took a long while as we had to go through a lot of villages first, but it was a pretty journey.

Doctors in those days didn't believe in herbal remedies and herbalists were regarded by the medical profession at that time as charlatans. There was no National Health Service then and you had to pay to go to the doctor.

My Mum told me a story of her having an abscess under her arm when she was a teenager and Grandma was very worried as it was very large and Mum was feeling quite poorly, so eventually she called in the doctor.

Now before this, Grandma had given Mum some ointment to try which she had got from the herbalist and this was on a table at the side.

When the doctor walked in, he saw the ointment, picked it up and threw it across the room, saying "Don't ever use that rubbish!!". The top flew off and ointment shot out, what a mess. The doctor was very angry at Grandma for having it in the house!

However, Grandma continued to visit her herbalist and used his healing ointments and medicines for many, many years.

There was a time when we are never sure to this day, if a herbal remedy saved my Dad's life or not.

Dad had been taken very ill, but didn't go into hospital because the doctor said he would be best at home with Mum looking after him. Dad had a duodenal ulcer. Now these days this is fairly easy to treat and it is uncommon for anyone to die from it, but in those days it was a very big worry.

Mum did all the doctor said, feeding Dad with all the right things and generally doing everything possible. Well, one day the doctor visited and told Mum that he was really sorry, but he didn't think Dad would last until the morning!

Oh my goodness, what dreadful news! What would we do if my Dad did die?

When the doctor had gone, Mum called me and through her tears, which she was trying desperately to hold back from me, said would I run as fast as I could and fetch my Grandma Bramley, who live about 15 minutes away if you ran.

I ran like a thing possessed, I am sure I must have broken records! When I got to Grandma's and told her what the doctor had said, she gave me a box of something called Slippery Elm and said to run fast back with it and tell Mum to give Dad some straight away. She would follow in a while.

So again, I flew as fast as my little legs would take me, with my heart thumping so loud (I am sure it wasn't just the exertion of running), with this box back home and told Mum what Grandma had said.

Mum immediately mixed up this Slippery Elm and fed some to Dad and Grandma came shortly after and stayed the night, both her and Mum sitting up with Dad. I had the job of looking after my sister if she woke up (she was asleep in her cot by this time).

The next morning, the doctor visited and Dad sat up in bed and joked with him, "Well, I am ready for my bacon and egg now doctor". The doctor could hardly believe the change in Dad. Mum told him about the Slippery Elm and he ridiculed any idea of that helping and said it was just nature and Dad had a strong constitution!

So what did we believe? It was very hard not to believe the herb had anything to do with Dad's recovery, but who is to say.

Dad duly recovered, but rigidly watched what he ate as he was told it could reoccur one day if he wasn't careful.

Many years later, when I was a teenager, the ulcer did come back and burst. Dad was then rushed into hospital and had an operation, after which he was completely fine.

Twenty Four

I loved to write when I was young
Would write all day once I'd begun
One day I did the writing square
Oh dearie me, how did I dare..................................

I really enjoyed my time at my primary school with the exception of one particular day. This was a day I threw caution to the winds and indulged in a bit of temper.

We had to write an essay. This was my favourite subject, I just loved to tell stories and really that's what an essay was.

Now, I prided myself on writing nicely and neatly and so set to, merrily writing away, when, all of a sudden the teacher was at my desk. I looked up to see what was wrong (something had to be or he wouldn't be standing there, or so I reasoned). Then the unbelievable happened - he said I was to improve my handwriting because it was becoming messy!

Although I was only eight years old then, I was really put out. Looking back now with hindsight, although usually my writing was neat and tidy, I think I may have got excited with my story and scribbled more than usual. Of course, I didn't think of that at the time. I just felt insulted.

So what to do? I was in a temper by then although I didn't let anyone know. Ok then, little madam that I was, I decided if he thinks that isn't good enough, let's see what he thinks of this. Of course, I didn't say that, I may have been foolhardy, but I wasn't stupid!

What did I do? I will tell all. I just said "yes sir" to the teacher, then proceeded to write in neat little squares. For example, an a became a little square box with a tail on, and a b would be a vertical line with a square at the end. I continued making every letter I wrote in the same fashion, and oh boy, did I ever regret it.

It took absolutely ages to write that essay, but I wouldn't give in. I was too stubborn. Because we had until the next day to finish, I took mine home with me to finish it.

When I gave that essay in the next day, the teacher just looked at me for a long while, and then didn't say a word.

Needless to say, I have never tried such a thing since but I did take a great deal of care with my handwriting after that.

I did practice different styles though and I have always enjoyed writing even in these days of computers, although these days my fingers ache after a while! Wouldn't fancy doing 100 lines now!!

Strangely enough, when I was much older, I joined a group to learn specialised handwriting, my favourite being old English, in which I discovered I had some skill.

This was to stand me in good stead in later years when I made and decorated wedding and birthday cakes. I enjoyed writing on the cakes in a fancy style.

Maybe I should have thanked that early teacher for starting something I was to later enjoy! I would have loved to have met up with him to see what on earth he made of the funny stubborn little girl in his class that day.

Twenty Five

What caused one granny to get in a huff?
The other one, well she would take snuff!
What a strange thing for her to do
Well as a child that was my view

She said it helped to clear her nose
She could be right, I do suppose...................

I have mentioned earlier that my two sets of grandparents were very different, well I think my Grandma Bramley was quite shocked at my Grandma Ratcliffe sometimes, although she never said anything. When Grandma Bramley was displeased with anything, she would draw her lips in tight. I always knew that look.

Well my Grandma Ratcliffe took snuff!! As a young child I didn't really place any importance to this (although I couldn't see the sense in it), it was just something this Grandma did. It is surprising how accepting children can be of things. Sometimes she would ask me to go to the shop where it was on sale to buy her some.

This shop really was fascinating. There was snuff in every colour and strength you could imagine. I hadn't realised that so many people took it. I knew my Dad did, and Mum used to say it was horrible and made all his handkerchiefs stained. Mum would keep a special bucket to soak Dad's hankies in and boiled them separately from everything else. Thank goodness he stopped in later years.

The snuff Grandma took was a fine white powder and it didn't seem to stain her hankies at all. She would put a tiny pinch on the back of one hand and then sniff it with a big sniff!! Very strange behaviour!

I remember feeling quite important trotting off to the shop to buy Grandma's snuff and although nobody ever said to me, I instinctively knew not to mention it to anyone else, especially not Grandma Bramley.

When I stayed at Grandma Ratcliffe's house for a while, she would make me have a rest in the afternoon. There was a big range in her living room and in the recesses either side of the fireplace a seat had been made. Grandma had made padded cushions to sit on and I had to lay down on one of them and was supposed to have a nap.

Now, I don't think I ever did more than pretend to sleep, I was too energetic and didn't want to sleep in the daytime. I began to suspect that if I had a nap, then Grandma could as well. When I was settled down, Grandma would sit in a high backed chair and close her eyes. Many's the time I though she was asleep and very, very gently eased myself off the seat, taking ages so I would be really quiet, but every time Grandma would open her eyes and I had to get back again. I never, ever escaped that afternoon nap until I was older and I was allowed to go out to the park, which was called 'the reccy'.

Oh how I loved that reccy. It was by the canal, and I loved to go on the swings and go so, so high, where I could see canal boats coming down. They would sometimes be very pretty and colourful, but quite often they would be dirty looking. If I went really high, I could see lots of things. I would spend literally hours swinging backwards and forwards.

There were bowls being played at the other end of the reccy, and I liked to stand and watch them. It didn't seem very exciting to me, but a lot of people used to play. There were several bowling greens and I used to like to walk up and down and see the different people playing. It seemed to me that nobody was playing the same as each other!

There were two entrances to the reccy. One was at the end of Grandma's road and the one I was supposed to use. The other was at the other end and led to the High Street. I wasn't really supposed to use this entrance, but sometimes I did. My Uncle Harold had a shoe shop there and if he saw me going by, I would be in trouble for not using the other entrance. Luckily for me, he was so often busy with customers I could run quickly by and not be spotted.

I loved it when I stayed there and my Uncle Jim would come in from work. He was about 10 years younger than my Dad and didn't get married until I was older.

Uncle Jim worked as a miner on the coal face and used to come home all dirty with coal soot. In those days, they didn't have baths or showers at the mines and Uncle would come home on the bus, all filthy with soot. He would pull funny faces at me with his black face and when he moved his mouth it looked white against the black!

First thing he did was to have a bath in the kitchen. The tin bath would be filled for him and the kitchen was out of bounds until Uncle Jim had finished and was all lovely and clean again.

Uncle worked down the mines for many years. It was very hard work indeed. I didn't envy him down in that dark place deep under the ground. He used to get a coal allowance which he gave to Grandma. Of course when he got married later on, he kept that for him and his own family. I know Grandma missed that.

Grandma Ratcliffe's was another place we would all have a sing song around the piano. My Auntie Lilian could play the piano, and whoever happened to be there at the time (and there were always several people around) would join in a song. A lot of fun and laughter there.

One thing I loved there which Mum didn't do at home was Yorkshire pudding with jam on for afters. Grandma used to make a very big Yorkshire pudding to go with the dinner and if there was some left over (there usually was), we would have it for pudding with jam. I loved that. It was always home made jam, very often some I had brought with me from Grandma Bramley who used to make a lot with her own plums.

I never really knew why Mum didn't have that for pudding at home because we would have it with roast beef, but there was never any over for a pudding.

I remember one time I was staying at Grandma Ratcliffe's when we were invited to a lady's house at the other end of the road to Grandma. This was a posh part of the road, where the houses were bigger and they had really big gardens. This lady had bought an 'ice box' from America.

Now, I had never heard of such a thing. There were no fridges then. We used to keep milk cool in the summer in a bucket of cold water with a piece of muslin over it, with the muslin soaking in the cold water. We also kept meat in a 'meat safe' on the wall outside the kitchen door. This would have a mesh front and was supposed to keep the meat cool. It was always situated in the shady part as near to the back door as possible.

So when I heard about an ice box, my imagination started working overtime. What on earth was it like? Well this lady invited all the children who lived in that street or as in my case, were visiting, round to have some home made ice cream. We all thought she must be very rich!

All of us children gathered around and, plucking up courage, because we were all a bit apprehensive about what we would find there. It is amazing how scared we all were. Anyway round we went and saw this big ice box. I remember it was a huge big thing but when the lady (I'm afraid I don't recall her name) opened it up, it was only quite small inside.

We were all given some ice cream in little dishes with spoons. It didn't look like ice cream I had seen before! What was it going to taste like? One brave child took a spoonful and smiled, so we all followed his lead and tasted it. It didn't taste like any ice cream I had had before from the ice cream van, but it was very nice.

We all finished our portion of ice cream and went away full of wonderment that somebody could make ice cream! I know you could make cakes and lots of other things that you could buy in the shops, but had never heard of anybody making ice cream. That was one very kind lady and I have never forgotten that ice cream.

Twenty Six

Shirley was crying and making a fuss
What could I do but catch the bus
Our poor Grandmas were in a state
And I climbed over the garden gate......................

I mentioned earlier how my sister and I would go to different grandparents during school holidays. This suited us both as we had made friends in both places, and meant the two sets of grandparents shared their grandaughters. We didn't always stay at the same place but swapped around.

I think this was good for us, because we both had a chance to experience different life styles. It also made it less stressful for the grownups to only have one child at a time. There was quite a large age gap really between my sister and I, which did narrow considerably as we grew older when we became best friends. However the younger you are the larger the gap seems. Shirley always wanted to do the same things I was doing, and obviously a lot of things I wanted to do just wasn't suitable for her, so this restricted my activities when we were together.

I didn't mind too much, because I did love my baby sister, but it was nice to be away sometimes and do the things I wanted to do without worrying about Shirley.

Grandma and Grandad Bramley lived in Loughborough a few streets away from our own home. The other grandparents lived in Syston near to Leicester. There was approximately 10-11 miles between the two places, but in those days we always went by bus. This journey could take quite a long while (or so it seemed to me), but it depended which bus you caught.

One bus didn't take too long because it went pretty much straight there, but if you had to get the other one, it would take you through all kinds of little villages and, although a pretty route, would take a lot longer.

On one occasion, when I was nine, I was staying at Grandma Ratcliffe's and Shirley was staying at Grandma Bramley's, and Grandma Bramley decided to bring Shirley over for a visit. Although both grandparents were quite different, they did get on quite well, and Grandma Ratcliffe was pleased to see Grandma Bramley and Shirley.

We all had a nice time together and I took Shirley exploring places I liked to go to. We went to the Reccy and on the swings as well. Grandma Ratcliffe got a nice tea for us all and then before we knew it, it was time for them to catch the bus back to Loughborough.

Oh dear, this is when trouble began! Shirley didn't want to leave me. She wanted to stay where I was. Well neither Grandmas would entertain the idea, so even though Shirley was crying her eyes out, they had to get ready and go to the bus stop.

I went with them to wave them off, and will never, ever forget that little face looking at me from the back of the bus as it drove away! There were tears streaming down Shirley's face and you could see she was sobbing!

This was too much for me, I couldn't have my baby sister so upset. I would have to do something about it! Back to Grandma

Ratcliffe's house I went, and said I was catching the next bus after them to be with my sister. I had never been so defiant before, but the sight of Shirley in the back of the bus well, I was undone..........

Looking back, I think Grandma Ratcliffe realised the best way to deal with this, because it must have become obvious to her that I would go my own way in any case, rather than letting me just go off, was to talk to me and make sure I really did know what I was doing.

I know I was only nine, but I was a very confident and independent young lady, also very determined. We had quite a long chat and eventually, she gave me the money for the bus fare and her blessing. I was sorry to leave her, but my sister needed me.

So off I skipped to catch the bus to Loughborough. I was like an anxious mum, couldn't wait to see my sister and give her a big hug. It seemed so important that I did this and it felt like the bus was taking forever.

Eventually, the bus stop where I had to get off arrived and off I ran (not even walking) to Grandma Bramley's house. Well! Guess what? I had arrived before them! The house was all locked up with nobody home.

It dawned on me that I must have been on the quick bus and they must have caught the one that went all through the villages.

What was I to do? I was tired and hungry, also anxious about Shirley. There was a side gate that led to the back garden which was also locked, so after a little thought, I climbed up and over it. Now Grandma and Grandad had fruit trees in the garden and there was a lovely Victoria plum tree. Fortunately for me, it was the time of the year when the plums were ready for picking. So up the plum tree I went and was sitting there, up the tree eating plums, when Grandma arrived back with Shirley.

My goodness me! What a surprise for them! It was a good job Grandma had a strong healthy heart! Not long ago she had said goodbye to me and left me standing at the roadside waving goodbye, and when she got home, there I was, to say she was amazed would be an understatement!

After all the tearful explanations, and my joyful reunion with my sister, it was Milo (a bedtime drink Grandma always gave us) and bed for us both.

I was so grateful to both Grandma's for being so understanding and not scolding me. I spent the rest of the time at Grandma Bramley's making sure Shirley behaved and doing all I could to be a good grandaughter, to show how grateful I was.

When I think back now, what trust my Grandma Ratcliffe had in me to allow me to go off like that. There were no telephones then to check I got there ok and she must have gone through an agony until she knew I was safe. In those days, you waited for a policeman to call to let you know if there was any kind of disaster. Grandma must have watched and waited anxiously praying she wouldn't see a policeman coming to her door.

My sister and I both remembered that time when, in recent years, she was really ill (she died shortly after) and phoned for me to go to her. I always loved her so dearly, as I know she loved me. We drifted apart over the years, busy with bringing up children etc, but saw each other quite often and in later years became close again as when we were children, only this time we really were grown up friends.

Twenty Seven

Time to move on and go to new places
Make new friends and see some new faces
Play on a windmill and run by the sea
Live in a toy shop, how good it can be

There was just one thing that did make me quake
For soon there would be two exams to take
I knew I shouldn't do it and take that sweet
But you see I simply wouldn't be beat................

Our time at Loughborough would soon be coming to an end. I didn't realise at the time but we went on holiday to Lytham St Annes, near to Blackpool, and Mum and Dad used this holiday to look for somewhere to live.

We stayed in a boarding house run by a lady called Mrs Standon, who I was told to call Auntie Standon. Of course I didn't realise at the time, but Auntie Standon was due to be looking after my sister and me, while Mum and Dad were looking for property.

It was as well she was a nice lady (but of course Mum would have known she was), because we did spend a lot of that holiday with her. Auntie Standon got me interested in a form of embroidery. This was a sort of cross between sewing and weaving. She would buy a great big (well I thought it was big) white cotton floor cloth and with a large needle threaded with wool, take the needle in and out of the cotton strands that made up the cloth. You alternated where you put the needle on each row you did.

We used different coloured wools every so often and when we had covered all the cloth with pretty patterns with the different wool, Auntie Standon showed me how to sew some material on the back to make a cushion cover. I actually loved doing this, although I was inclined to get a bit frustrated because I wanted to finish too quickly so I would have a cushion cover, and sometimes had to undo what I had done, because I was rushing it. Typical me, not sure if I have changed that much!

Shirley just played with bits of wool while I was doing this with Auntie Standon. I had shown her how to make little fluffy balls by winding wool around two cardboard milk bottle tops, the ones that used to have a hole in the middle. You kept winding and winding until you couldn't get any more wool round, then cut through the two milk bottle tops, wrapped a strand of wool round the middle, removed the milk bottle tops and you had a fluffy little ball.

Thankfully, we did get to spend time with Mum and Dad, doing normal holiday things like sandcastles on the beach etc. One thing I loved to do if I got the chance, was to go to the windmill that was there in Lytham.

I would climb up on to the platform that goes around the base and run round and round the windmill. I thought it was a marvellous thing. I know the windmill is still there, but strongly suspect it will be protected these days from little girls running round and round it, trying to leap up and peer in the windows!

I would stand on the side facing the sea, letting my imagination run riot. If I lived there, in the windmill, what would it be like? I could go to the top and watch the ships going along. As I was frequently told at school, my head was always in the clouds!

If I could wangle it, I would escape and go exploring on my own. I loved nothing better than to go down all the different streets to see what was there. I didn't find a reccy like the one at Grandma Ratcliffe's though. Strangely, I never did find a reccy like that in all the different places we were to live over the years.

I even went down to the shops and investigated what there was. Of course, I was always in trouble when I got back for going off on my own, but that was a price I was willing to pay for the freedom of exploring. I have to say, I always took note of where I was and never spoke to anyone, just looked at things that seemed interesting. I never understood how that was being naughty.

I must have liked what I saw, because later on, after we had returned home, I was excited when Mum told me we would be moving to go and live in Lytham. I was to miss my friend Margaret, we had been friends since we moved to Parklands Drive and always went to school together, but the excitement of moving and to a seaside of all places just took precedence.

I didn't know then but an uncle of my Mum's had died and left her some money, so both my parents decided they wanted to try their hand at running a shop.

So we went to live above Ratcliffe's Toy Shop (Ratcliffe being my maiden name). This was a large, narrow, 3 storied house in the Georgian style, and also a large attic that had been made into 2 bedrooms. The front ground floor room was the shop.

The first floor was where we had our sitting room and kitchen, Mum and Dad had a bedroom on the second floor and Shirley and myself had our bedrooms in the attic. This was great for us, we had a whole floor to ourselves! We really thought it was fantastic. I liked to look through the skylight at the stars at night. We did have windows as well, and thought this was great.

Just imagine, living with a toy shop in your front room!! A child's heaven! Except of course, we weren't allowed to touch anything, so we soon lost interest in that!!

It did get more interesting later on, when Dad decided to have a Dolls Hospital, where he repaired broken dolls for children. I used to sit and watch him put arms back on and all kinds of things to make the dolls good again.

It was great that we had the beach almost on our doorstep! Actually, it was just across a road and a short walk. I was fascinated with the sea and loved to just watch the waves. Collecting sea shells was another thing I loved and made all kinds of pretty things with them.

We went to the local school but it wasn't long before I would be moving on because it would soon be time for me to take the eleven plus or the scholarship as it was sometimes called.

The day of the exam dawned. I was very nervous, what would it be like? Well, I duly took the exam with all the various papers and found the questions not too difficult, but my problem was, I took a long while over the questions. I would put in the answer and then read it again. I was so afraid I had got it wrong. The result was that I didn't complete all the papers. I was mortified!! Now I would be bound to fail! Why hadn't I trusted myself and moved on quicker!

This unfortunately, is something that has always been a problem to me, even now. I have to revisit things to make sure I have them right!

So the wait for results began. Then round it came, results were here. Guess what? I had passed!!! Apparently, although I hadn't completed every paper, all the answers I had given were correct, so although I was given a pass, it was marked 'borderline'. Whew, better than I expected!!

However, it wasn't all over, I had one more exam to take! This was an entrance exam to the Queen Mary High School and everyone had to sit this if they wanted to go there.

Now whether I had more confidence then as I had just sat the first real exam in my young life or not I don't know, but I found this exam, although hard, easier than the eleven plus. I had learnt my lesson about not hesitating with my answers and finished every paper actually ahead of time.

Because I am 'me' and things cannot ever (even now at my advanced age) run as smoothly as they should (usually my fault), there had to be a glitch!! Sweets were forbidden when you sat this exam, but of course I had to take a sweet with me. I reasoned (I was good at that!) that if I wasn't rustling paper opening a sweet, nobody would know, so I took one single pear drop, all ready to pop in my mouth, in my blazer pocket.

I had finished one of the papers ahead of time and thought, right, time for my sweetie, so popped the pear drop in my mouth. Fine, I was enjoying it when all of a sudden, I swallowed wrongly (you know how you can) and the sweet somehow became stuck in my throat! Oh my goodness! What to do? Now I don't know if you have ever tried to choke quietly, but it isn't the easiest thing to do!! I had one eye on the lady supervising us and desperately tried to swallow this wretched pear drop.

Eventually I succeeded, and could breathe a sigh of relief. For about two hours afterwards though, I had a sore throat where it had been stuck. It felt as if it was still there! Oh well, lesson learnt, I did pass that exam and nobody ever knew about the pear drop! You, my readers are the first to know! You won't be surprised to know I don't like pear drops these days!!

Lytham Windmill

Twenty Eight

I'm a big girl now off to a big school
I had better be good, not break any rule
Please tell me why I should wear a hat
I mean, must I really and truly wear that?

Well I meant to be good and tried for a while
But when I was naughty I did it in style
I tried to make the school really smell
Then swung from the beams in the ceiling as well................

So, now I was all set to go to my new school. Uniform to get was the next step. Oh my goodness! I found I had to wear a hat!! Really! Do I have to?? Oh yes, I had to!

Now I had a nice new uniform with a pretty summer dress and a tunic for the winter. That was all fine but oh those hats!! There was a felt hat that I thought looked like a pudding for the winter and horror of horrors - a straw hat that looked like a boater for the summer! I couldn't possibly go out in those things could I??? Oh yes, I could!

It did feel a bit better when I was in the company of other girls going to my school, but if I was on my own, I would whip whichever hat it was off my head and stick it in my bag! I was lucky a teacher or prefect didn't catch me because I would have got a conduct point.

Getting one conduct point wasn't too bad, but you had to be careful because if you had three conduct points in one term, you then had a detention point. This was bad. You would likely go before a prefects court if you had one. I came very close on two occasions, both in the same term.

Much as I hate to admit it (although my friends won't be in the least bit surprised), I could get up to mischief! One time I was in big trouble, but escaped with just one conduct point, was when I made the whole school smell of rubber!

It was like this..........the classroom I was in at the time was an old building apart from the main block. It was quite large and had lovely beams in the ceiling. It also had a boiler which heated the radiators for the whole school. It was always lovely and warm in there. One day, someone in my class said if we put some rubber in the boiler it would smell all through the school.

Did I need a better invitation to get up to mischief? Naturally not! My friend and I went off searching in the sand dunes (our school was set very close to the sand dunes near Blackpool) until we found part of a rubber tyre. Perfect!! When the opportunity arose i.e: when our teacher disappeared, we both put a piece of the rubber tyre into the boiler.

Nothing happened for a while, then all of a sudden there was this smell!! All of our class was in hysterics. We couldn't stop laughing! Of course there was an inquiry because our teacher wasn't stupid (even though we liked to think so) and the end result, my friend and I confessed because otherwise it meant the whole class would be punished.

Well I decided I had better be good. I didn't like getting conduct marks. Unfortunately, my good intentions didn't last long.

Now I was quite agile, as lots of youngsters are, and had been used to climbing trees where I used to live, and had long had an ambition to be a trapeze artist (the idea of being a missionary had faded by now). Something, at the time I regretted (but now am very glad) my parents didn't share this ambition. However, whenever an opportunity arose to swing upside down, I took it and became quite adept at it.

Actually when I think now, it is a pity nobody spotted the potential of a gymnast in me, although if they had I don't believe there were opportunities then to foster it.

Anyway there I was in this classroom that had these lovely beams on the ceiling!! I looked and looked at them every day, all the time thinking, I wish! Naturally, I had to do it one day and the day came. Our teacher was called to the main school for some reason and we were given some reading to do.

Yes, I did read for a while, but eventually the temptation became too great and with the encouragement of the whole class I clambered onto the desk top and jumped until I caught hold of a beam and I was away! After swinging normally with my hands on the beam, I managed to hang by my feet and swing backwards and forwards, showing off for all I was worth! It was fantastic, I was in heaven! Until...........

The door opened a voice screamed out 'Ann Ratcliffe, what are you doing?' Oh dear oh dear, how I didn't fall straight to the ground I will never know! I hadn't been so scared in my life! Why did she come back so early, why couldn't she have stayed away a bit longer!

So the end of this was, after a disciplinary talk from the head, I had yet another conduct mark! Oh Ann you must behave now, it is coming dangerously close to getting three!

When I look back, I was fortunate not to have had more in my time at that school because a group of us would go down the fields and behind the sand dunes and we could see the boys in the school next door playing rugby. This was totally forbidden, but we did it anyway. Wonder of wonders, I was never caught.

I think maybe it was a good idea that my parents moved house and I had to leave and go to another school!

One happy memory of my time living in Lytham was reporting on a football match for my Dad.

I didn't know at the time, but Dad was struggling with the business. Trade wasn't as good as it could be. When I was older I realised that the venture was doomed to failure from the start. Lovely as my Dad was, one thing he wasn't, and that was a business man. Anyway, I never knew the ins and outs, but for a time Dad did his best to keep it going. To help with financial problems Dad took on a job as a sports reporter for the local paper. This was only part time as he was still running the shop with Mum's help.

Actually, I know Dad enjoyed this reporting lark and I believe he was good at it. One day, he had a dilemma! There were two football matches at the same time on the same Saturday that Dad wanted to cover, so he called in the Troops, little me!! I believe I was twelve at the time and so proud to do this for my Dad. I went to one match and noted down who scored which goal and any things that stood out.

When the match was finished, I went outside to a phone box and told Dad the details so he could pass them on to the paper. That was it, no longer did I want to be trapeze artist, it was a reporter for me!!

In fact, it wasn't to be long before we were off somewhere new.

Twenty Nine

Poor little bird, please don't die, nor you dear little mouse
I'll look after you in my hospital, just behind the house
I will nurse you and feed you and help you get well
I will do my best for you as I think you can tell

That wasn't successful, it was such a shame
I really did try, it wasn't a game
So what can I do to do good in this world
Well read a bit more, my plans are unfurled................

When we lived in Lytham we didn't have a garden, just a large back yard with storage sheds for the shop. That was still big enough for Shirley and me to play in, so we didn't mind too much not having a garden. The back yard was big enough to have friends round to play and we were allowed to use one of the sheds to play in as well.

Many a little play was put on in that shed and it was a great place for make-believe for my sister. It also became a place where

I tried to make animals better! I found an injured bird once and decided to heal it. I went to the shoe shop round the corner and asked if I could have a shoe box. They kindly gave me a couple and I took them back home and found some of Shirley's dolls (I wasn't playing with dolls then, being a big girl!) blankets from her pram, lined the box and put this poor little sparrow in. I got some milk and dipped a tiny piece of bread in and fed it to the bird. He did manage to eat it but unfortunately, it wasn't long before it died. I was devastated because I thought with love and kindness it might get better and live.

After that, there were a couple more birds (friends were bringing in one if they found it) and even one mouse!! Now I was always afraid of mice (still not too happy) but this poor little thing had managed to escape next doors cat and it looked at me with such sad eyes and he could hardly move. So I overcame my fear and put it in one of my shoe boxes of which I had a collection by now.

The tender loving care began and Shirley had instructions to keep the cat away, but of course to no avail and the little mouse went the way of the birds.

So my future as a vet wasn't to be.

Next thing I decided to do (somehow I was determined to help someone!) was raise money and give to our local hospital. I don't know why I thought the hospital should be helped and not somewhere else, maybe a grownup had mentioned they needed more money, I don't know.

Anyway, I made a plan. I would hold a Jumble Sale in our back yard. I checked with Mum and she just smiled and said go ahead and gave me some stuff to put on my stall. Then I set about organising things in the yard. Now I needed more things to sell, this wasn't enough, so I thought I would go to some of the houses near by and ask if they had any things they didn't want. I would explain what I wanted it for and hopefully it would be ok.

Then I had a thought. Oh dear, would I be breaking the law? I was uncertain about some laws and didn't know if I would be allowed to ask for and then sell things like that. Did I have to have a licence or something? Was I too young to be allowed to sell?

Mum hadn't said anything about it, I could check with her. No, I didn't want to pester her because she was very busy. Only thing for it, off to the Police Station and ask. I couldn't get into trouble for asking could I? No, surely not.

So although I was nervous, never having been in a police station before and not really knowing what to expect, I plucked up my courage and went round there. I felt a bit shaky going in but the policeman sitting at the counter smiled encouragement at me and asked me how he could help.

This was alright, I could speak to him, he seemed a nice man. So I told him of My Plan and he smiled and reassured me it would be ok for me to do that. Oh I was on cloud nine. Not only had I done something I was a bit scared about, I would be able to carry out My Plan with no fear of getting into trouble! I have since thought that policeman probably had a chuckle with his mates in the canteen later at this little girl coming in and asking an unusual question! Thank you Mr Policeman for making a little girl's day, although it is pretty certain you won't be reading this!

Now came the next stage of this Master Plan, off round houses to ask for contributions of jumble! As it turned out people were very kind and obliging and I collected a motley assortment of stuff. By the way, I didn't tell Mum I was going round houses like that, I secretly thought she wouldn't approve so I reasoned if I didn't ask permission, but just did it, it would be ok.

So back to the yard and one last thing to do before opening the gate at the side of the shop which led to the yard, and that was to make a sign advertising the Jumble Sale.

Cardboard was found and colouring pencils and with Shirley's help, I produced a sign saying 'Jumble Sale in aid of the Hospital here today at 3 o'clock'.

We were a little disappointed with the attendance, not very many people came in to buy, but some did and we made some money for the hospital, but not as much as I had hoped for. If I remember correctly, it was about six shillings and two pence that I proudly took round to the hospital. I don't think they knew what to do with it! This wasn't something that they were used to have happening. However, a very nice lady thanked me for my trouble and said it would be put to good use. I have no idea what she did with it, but I went home feeling very virtuous.

Mum and Dad never, ever knew the full story about going round houses and to the police station.

That was my one and only venture into raising money for charity in this way!! I didn't think I wanted to do that for a living when I was grown up. It wasn't so easy trying to help people after all.

It was while we were living in Lytham, Shirley had appendicitis and had to have her appendics out. Unfortunately, I can't remember the name of the hospital she stayed in for her operation, but it had nice grounds. Visiting in hospitals was very strict in those days and I wasn't allowed in to visit. To get round this, I found out where the nearest window to Shirley's bed was and went round on the grass to talk through the window.

One time we were visiting and Mum and Dad had gone into the ward and I went round to the window again, when all of a sudden, Mum started to laugh and was beckoning me to go nearer to the window. Mum then put her head outside and passed me a book. In between chuckling, Mum said would I shake the book upside down and see what happened. I did that and then started to laugh myself! What came out was a load of cabbage!! Shirley wouldn't eat cabbage at all and I suppose the hospital insisted she did, so she hid it in pages of books!

That was another source of hilarity in our grown-up years! Another hiding place Shirley used when she was at home for anything she didn't like, was the staves under the dining table! When Mum went to clean under there, she would find little crusts of bread and suchlike!

Thirty

Well here we go, we're off again
Will this be where we may remain?
It's rooms this time and there is someone
Who gets in touch with those who are gone

It's only a while that we stay there
Where next you may think, goodness me where?
It's like this you see, my Dad knows a man
Who will let us stay in his caravan..................

So the time came again when it was time to move. This time not because Dad wanted another job, but because the business floundered. So Dad had got another job back in his old trade of proof reading.

One advantage my sister and I had with Dad being a proof reader, we learnt very early how to spell and even knew the Latin that some words came from, because as well as it being Dad's job, the English Language was his hobby. He loved words and liked to find out the origin of some words and encouraged us both. Even now, I find myself thinking of Dad when I am spelling a particularly difficult word.

Anyway, back to the move. This time we were off to Oxford. For once, I wasn't so excited because I had not long settled into my new school and didn't relish the idea of starting again. I thought long and hard and then went to have a TALK with Mum and Dad.

I had done what Dad had always taught me, if I was going to put my case to someone, I must prepare. Think carefully about what I was going to say, and have my arguments in my mind. So, I approached them with hope that I might get my way.

I had passed my eleven plus and gone to High School. Now I never really felt that I fitted in there. Teachers and pupils alike were friendly enough and I seemed to get on with everybody, however, most of them were, to my eyes and ears, posh! I didn't like how pupils had crushes on older pupils and prefects. I thought it was stupid, some of them would act as if they were in love or something. No, this really wasn't for me!

I knew if I stayed in High School I would have to stay at school until I was sixteen but if I went to a Secondary Modern, I could leave at fifteen. So, I reasoned if I went to Secondary Modern I could leave and go to work earlier and I wouldn't have to keep changing schools. I had no great ambitions at the time, maybe work with children or something in newspapers. We were still in the era where girls got married and gave up work to bring up children. Although some women did work as my Mum worked in the shop.

So I put my thoughts and feelings to Mum and Dad and asked when we moved could I please go to a Secondary Modern school instead of a High School. Well, the talking went on for a long while, but Dad had taught me well how to conduct an argument, and eventually it was agreed. They did know of a good school near where we were going. Now I was happy about the move and looked forward to my new school.

This was to be a school called Temple Cowley in Cowley, Oxford. I have since found out that this school was knocked down in 2003. I don't have any particular memories of that school, as it was destined we would move again shortly, although I enjoyed it and I believe did quite well.

When we reached Oxford, we had to stay in lodgings because the house that went with the job wasn't yet ready. I think there was a problem with the present occupiers moving out. So we stayed with this very nice lady, Shirley and I sharing a bedroom. I didn't mind staying there but it was only for a very short time. It was a little spooky living there as the lady who the house belonged to was a medium and would hold séances there in her front room.

She got it into her head that I was receptive to the spirit world which I found a bit scary, as she used to ask me things like did I dream and other stuff that I thought was very strange. So I suppose I wasn't altogether unhappy when it was time for us to leave there.

We moved then into a caravan situated on some land belonging to a builder. It was very cramped in the caravan and not really very nice, although as usual, Mum and Dad made everything fun and we laughed a lot. Our parents could always see the funny side of things which, all things considered, was probably just as well. We also had a funny incident when my sister Shirley, accidentally put her foot through the side of the wardrobe!! We slept in bunk beds and these were fitted in between a cupboard at the head and a wardrobe at the bottom. One night, Shirley must have been dreaming. All of a sudden there was a sort of crashing sound! We discovered Shirley's foot had gone straight through the wardrobe! We none of us could help laughing, although it cost Mum and Dad money to have it repaired. Shirley and I recalled this incident in our grown up lives and used to laugh ourselves silly thinking about it!

I made friends with the builders daughter although she was a couple of years older than me. We spent quite a bit of time together and she taught me how to cut and file my nails in the way grown up girls did. I know this is not the fashion any longer, it is now square nails, but at that time it was pointed ones. I went home to Mum and showed her my little pointed nails very pleased with myself! I don't think Mum was as pleased as me somehow!

Anyway, our stay in the caravan was to be very brief, as was our stay in Oxford. I think the job Dad had taken wasn't as good as he thought it would be and the accommodation never materialised. For a while my parents weren't the happy, jokey people I knew.

The next move was going to be back in Leicestershire, actually in Leicester itself. It was like we were going home again! We were very excited as we prepared for the move. We did keep moving to different places, and although it wasn't always good, it was always exciting!

We wouldn't be far away from my Grandma Ratcliffe, so that would be nice. Come on, let's get packed and off again!!

Thirty One

Things are changing now, I'm no longer a child
I am growing up, and must not now be so wild
Sunday school to teach, and boyfriend to meet
Growing up is indeed quite a feat

Did I do right or did I do wrong
Should I have chosen the other one?
Did I choose well, was it the right one
Well it's too late now, that time has gone...............

So off we went. Look out Leicester, here we come! I was now on the point of leaving childhood behind and on the verge of going into that half child - half grown up stage that can be so difficult. I was beginning to feel grown up and yet wasn't. I was now a teenager though!! I expected to feel different when I reached thirteen, and was a little disappointed to really feel the same!

We were going to be living in a terrace house on Herschall Street. It seemed to be quite a nice place, nothing special but not bad. We didn't have a back garden there but now I was at a senior school and had to travel on the bus to it and home again, there didn't seem much time for playing in the back. Children used to play on the street, although I was actually leaving that behind me now, (seeing as I was a teenager!) and made friends with girls (and boys) who lived in the same street and we would go round each others houses or across to the park which was quite near.

This park was nothing like the old recce at Syston. It was very big and just had grass and flowerbeds. We used to go and sit on the seats and chatter.

A new school again, what would it be like? Would I enjoy it? Would I make new friends? The answers to all of the above questions is yes, yes and yes! This was a great school situated in Thurmaston called Roundhill, which is just outside of Leicester and not far from Syston where my Grandma Ratcliffe lived. I would go on the bus to school and quite often home to Grandma's at dinner time. Then home again on the bus in the evening.

I played hockey here for the first time. We had to cross the road as the playing field the school used for hockey, football etc was on the opposite side to the school. We also played netball, which I loved. I liked it better than hockey, and it wasn't long before I was in the school team. We used to practice a lot and I was very keen.

One other thing at this school was the choir. I was asked to join it and absolutely loved it. I willingly gave up dinner times to practice with the other choir members.

I think I must have picked up something from Mum, because I really loved singing. I would walk around the house at home singing away to myself. A habit that was to stay with me forever.

Of course, things never can run smoothly for very long! Just the way of things, I suppose. One day, I had a dilemma! What on earth was I to do? There was a final practice for an important netball match and a final practice for a concert the choir were putting on. Both were at the same time on the same day, and both teachers insisted I attend their own event!! Obviously, I couldn't do both. Which was my first love? The choir mistress said if I didn't attend this practice, then unfortunately I wouldn't be allowed to sing at the concert. The PE teacher said I would be letting the side down in this important match if I didn't attend this last training session!

Actually, in retrospect, when I look back, I am sure these two ladies could have found a solution if they had wished. However, I had to decide what to do. I went home worried who I would let down. For once, I didn't go to my Dad with this problem. Maybe it was a sign of adulthood being on the horizon, but I felt I had to deal with this on my own.

What did I decide? Did I regret it? Would I do it differently if I could go back in time? The answer to the first is, I chose netball. No, I think I chose the right thing because the choir could still perform with one less person, but the netball team couldn't. I know they could have brought someone else in, but I also knew that it would affect morale with the others in the team. Yes, I would do the same again. It was a very difficult decision.

As well as enjoying school, I also joined a youth group attached to the church. I didn't any longer attend church on a regular basis but this was like a youth club. Well through this group, I became a Sunday School teacher. Now this I really loved. I had a little group of about six or seven little children and would tell them a story from the bible, then I would get them to draw me a picture from the story. It was amazing how different they interpreted the story. They never drew from the same part of the story to each other.

One other thing that happened when I was living in Leicester was that I somehow managed to have a boyfriend. He was named Bruce and lived in the same street as me. We started to go for walks together and sometimes to the park. This was a very innocent relationship, we never did anything other than talk, but we seemed to share a lot of things. Bruce was interested in cars, well

I had never even thought about cars until I met him. We would sometimes sit in the park and watch cars go by (there was a main road we could see from the park). Bruce would say he could tell which car was coming before we could actually see it, and nine times out of ten, he would be right. So then we would talk about engine capacity etc. What you will do when you are in love!! You can tell this was a long while ago, when there were not many cars around in comparison to today.

One day I was offered a pet tortoise by a friend who didn't want it anymore, so I checked with Mum and she said it would be alright. He was lovely, and I made a bed for him. This was the first time I had had a pet of any description. Since I was bitten by Paddy at Grandma Bramley's when I was little, I hadn't thought about a pet. Having a tortoise was different to having a dog, and I really enjoyed him.

All in all I was enjoying my new life in Leicester. The days when I carried a tin of treacle on my head and sneaked into a bell foundry, seemed so long ago. I was at the age when I was beginning to see things with very different eyes.

Leicester itself was a very busy place. I found it fascinating. The other places we had lived in seemed very quiet in comparison. Everyone seemed to be rushing here and there as if they were all in a hurry. I wanted to be part of that rushing around. However, I really had enough in my life to keep me happy at that time.

I really enjoyed living in Leicester. It was also nice being a short bus ride to my Grandma Ratcliffe and just a little longer to Grandma and Grandad Bramley.

There was only one thing that marred this happiness, my Mum became ill. It was diagnosed that she had pleurisy and unfortunately, this was to plague her for many years to come.

The first time Mum had this was a little scary, because Mum was never ill and now she was very poorly. The doctor prescribed Kaolin poultice to be placed on her chest, and I learnt how to heat this and put it in the flannel that had to be put on Mum's chest, so

I could do it if Dad couldn't. Mum was very weak and had to stay in bed all the time. She recovered after a couple of weeks, but was still inclined to be weak. Dad, Shirley and I helped in whatever way we could.

Unfortunately, it did keep recurring during the winter months and I can remember going round to the chemist after hours and knocking them up to get some more Kaolin for Mum once when she became poorly and it was after hours. Luckily, the chemist lived above the shop and was able to come down, and because he knew Mum and her history of pleurisy was able to help.

Dad was a New Man before the term was invented! He loved to take a tray to Mum in bed and used to make things look so attractive. He would cut the bread in fancy shapes and if Mum had soup, Dad would make little croutons in funny shapes to float on the top. Best of all, if he could get hold of a flower, he would put it in a tiny vase on the tray. It always looked so nice.

Even when Mum was well, Dad would often help out with the housework to lighten the load for Mum. My sister and I were encouraged to help also, but were never made to. Both Mum and Dad had the belief that we should WANT to help, not be coerced. It might be suggested though, something would probably have been said to the effect 'I think your Mum might like a hand' or something similar. For this same reason we were never paid pocket money for jobs around the house. Dad used to say we should do it for the right reasons.

Thankfully, Mum did bounce back and was free of this for a couple of years. Mum had such a love of life, it was awful to see her poorly, although she always smiled and tried to make light of things.

Thirty Two

I heard one day, just by chance
There's going to be a special dance
It really wasn't a dance at all
But would be a Christmas Ball

Oh goodness me what would I wear
Would have to be special to go there
My Mum she got her dress in blue
And said, 'I'll make it right for you'

If you would like to know some more
Please read on, it won't be a chore............

A big highlight in the school year while I was at Roundhill, was the Christmas Ball. This was an amazing thing, I had never known anything like it before. It was a proper Ball where we were all expected to dress in formal evening wear, and all the teaching staff acted as waiters, waitresses, doormen, cloakroom attendants etc.

This was talked about for weeks beforehand. All the girls were deciding what they were going to wear. This was at the time when long dresses were worn on these occasions, and none of us girls had long dresses or only one or two anyway out of the whole school. The older girls had been before obviously, but us first year students were totally bewildered by all this.

Although I was excited, I was also secretly worried. I knew Mum and Dad didn't have a lot of money and I couldn't see how they would afford to buy me a new dress, not of the sort I would need anyway. It crossed my mind whether to develop an illness that would see me over the few days either side of the ball, but couldn't see how I would pull this off. Besides, I really did want to go.

I really needn't have worried, because as usual, my lovely Mum came up trumps yet again. I don't think she ever let me down. Anyway, Mum said she would make me a lovely dress out of the one I so loved when I saw her singing on the stage in the theatre years ago.

Mum was true to her word, and I think she had some help from Grandma Ratcliffe, but I was given this lovely dress to try on. Mum had cut some from the bottom as it was obviously too long for me, and used some of that to make the shoulder straps more suitable for a girl my age. They were originally very thin straps, now they had net gathered up and looked lovely. The dress had been altered to fit me, and I felt like a princess in it. Now I really could look forward to going to the Ball.

Now as the day approached, nerves started to kick in. How should I behave? What about dancing? I hadn't been to a dance before and this was more than a dance, it was a BALL! Even if I could dance, I was scared of dancing with a BOY!!

Oh well, at last the day arrived. I was staying at my Grandma Ratcliffe's because it was nearer and a group of us were walking to the school from Syston. Amazing when I think about it today, that would never happen now. Anyway, there I was, in my bed at my grandma's and my dress was hanging on the door all ready for me.

It was arranged that my friend Eileen would come round for me in plenty of time before we had to leave, so we could go round to her auntie's who was going to make us up. I was even more excited at this prospect, me with make up on!! Another step nearer to being grown up! We kept giggling and Eileen had to have her lipstick done again because she kept giggling and it smudged.

Eventually, there we were, all made up and ready to go. I can't begin to describe the feelings I had as we set out to walk to the Ball. Happy, sad, excited, shy, scared, all kinds of emotions all mixed up together.

Well we finally arrived at the door, and again, Eileen and I had the giggles to see the teachers dressed as waiters and waitresses, and we were all posh! When we had calmed down, we had a really lovely evening. I needn't have worried, everything was fine. The food was nice, although I don't think I realised what I was eating, and I did have a dance. In fact, I think I had three. The nice thing too, was how the teachers also joined in the fun with us, while still managing to retain our respect.

It was a very happy evening, and now it was nearing it's end. We got our coats and those of us who walked together, all collected up ready for the walk home. Now, as you may have gathered from my mention of Bruce earlier, I was just beginning to be aware of boys as something more than someone you climbed trees with! I can't remember for sure, but think there were three boys and four girls in our group to go home to Syston.

One of the boys lived near to my Grandma and as we got nearer to home, we sort of walked together. I was getting very nervous all over again. When I look back, I seem to have spent quite a bit of time being nervous! Mickey and I weren't boyfriend and girlfriend, just friends but we seemed to have suddenly gone from children on this magical night to while not yet grown up, certainly approaching that status. I started to think, 'what if he puts his arm around me', and what if he wants to kiss me'. Oh dear, the butterflies!

When we approached the end of Grandma's road, Mickey said 'it is still early, we don't have to be home just yet, lets go for a walk round the reccy'. I agreed and off we went. I had never walked round there in the dark, but I wasn't scared. It didn't seem creepy or anything and we talked and talked, ending up sitting on a bench still talking.

I needn't have worried, because Mickey was the perfect gentleman, and didn't attempt to do anything like putting his arm around me. I have wondered since if he was perhaps as nervous as me. Anyway, he eventually saw me home to my Grandma's and we said goodnight. I remember thanking him for walking me home and went in to see Grandma with a clear conscience and lots of happy things to tell her.

I gossiped to my Grandma for ages, telling her all about the ball and how we all giggled and were a bit noisy on the way home. I didn't mention the walk on the reccy though, that was my very special secret.

Mickey and I only saw each other occasionally after that as I lived in Leicester and we only really saw each other at school. I don't think it entered our heads to 'go out' together, very few of my friends had boyfriends in the proper sense of the word, and it was to be another two years before I did. It was just the magic of that special night, I think that made things seem different.

Thirty Three

Oh how exciting life could be
So much to do, so much to see
Go to the pictures and see Everest
And skating to do, that was the best

We went to stay at our grandparents home
We had to be good and couldn't roam
But I broke the rules and used a ploy
To go out with, good gracious, a boy................

One day at school, my class was told we would be going to the pictures in Leicester to see a documentary about the conquering of Mount Everest. Now I had heard about this amazing feat, but it didn't really mean that much to me then. I think at that time in my life my head was so much up in the clouds, that some things didn't really register on my radar screen. So I just thought it was interesting that we would be going, at that time it was a treat to go out of school for any reason.

All the trips and outings and journey's abroad with schools these days make our little trip to the local cinema seem very minor in comparison, but we were all quite excited.

It really was fascinating to watch with all the hardships that Edmund Hillary and Sherpa Tenzing went through, although our attention span maybe wasn't as good as it would be when we got older as we did get a bit bored when there seemed to be more talking than action in some parts, and we began to talk and got told off!

In the end though, it brought my head down from the clouds for a while! It really was amazing what they achieved, and I have to say, I really enjoyed it. Something to remember.

There was something else I remember about my time in Leicester and that was going roller skating in the De Montford Hall. Now in those days, girls didn't wear trousers that often, unlike today, and I wanted some to wear to go roller skating. My friends had started to wear them and it made sense for something like this, so Mum bought me a pair of brown trousers. I was over the moon and wore them the first time I went.

We had to queue for ages before we could go in and gradually I realised the inside of my legs were getting sore and chaffed with the unfamiliar trousers. I had never worn any before and was very uncomfortable that first time. Typically of a youngster of that age, I didn't say anything to anyone and just put up with it and as I kept wearing them, my legs got used to it and it was ok.

This was to be a regular thing every Saturday during the time I spent in Leicester. It seemed that so many new things were happening to me now, it was a little bewildering at times. I was fast approaching the age when I would want to go out in the evenings with friends and I think my parents had prepared for this very well. I don't ever remember being told I MUST be in at a certain time. Dad would say something like 'enjoy yourself and don't be too late'. I always knew that both Mum and Dad would be hurt if

I abused the trust they placed in me and tried my best not to let them down.

I couldn't bear to see the look on either of their faces if Shirley or me did, as was perfectly natural that we would occasionally do, in spite of our good intentions.

Anyway, it would seem that our time in Leicester was coming to an end. We would soon be moving on, this time to a place called Maidenhead, which was in Berkshire. Dad had got a job as a proof reader at a company called the Electrical Press and we were going to live in a new house which was still being built.

The school holidays were approaching and it was arranged that Shirley and myself would go and stay with Grandma Bramley until the new house was ready, which should be by the time term started again. One more new school!

Now since I last wrote about Grandma and Grandad Bramley, they had moved to live in Rhyl in Wales. They had a very nice bungalow with a garden. The garden was smaller than the one they had in Loughborough, but was quite nice. It was easier for them living in a bungalow now they were getting older. My once busy busy Grandma was slowing down. Age didn't stop them going out for long walks though.

As we were now both growing up, our Grandma could have us both together to stay which was good. We were also given a little more leeway. We still had to go to church twice on Sundays though.

I used to write to Bruce and one day he sent a letter to say he was coming to Rhyl for a holiday with his parents. We both hoped we could meet. Then the day came there was a knock on the door and it was Bruce. He wanted me to go to the fun fair with him, but unfortunately Grandma said no. She wasn't happy about me going off with a boy she didn't know. After all, I was in her care and I was also growing up!

As a consolation she let me bake some pastries for tea, as she knew I enjoyed baking cakes. However, I am sorry to say, this didn't stop me from being naughty. When I knew I couldn't go out, Bruce and I whispered that we would meet on Sunday and arranged where. I just hoped I could get away.

Sunday came round and for the first time in my young life, I lied to my beloved Grandma and Grandad. I said I wasn't feeling well and wouldn't be able to go to church in the evening! So I was allowed to stay at home while the others went off to church. As soon as they were gone, I got ready and went off to meet Bruce.

We had a lovely time, went on the racing cars and walked along the beach, then back home to Grandmas. It was all so very innocent and I was back in good time before them. I thought all would be well. Wrong!! Grandma had seen sand on my shoes and questioned me! I had to tell the truth then and felt so bad about it. I was forgiven but didn't meet Bruce again. In fact, I have never seen him since!

There was plenty to do while we stayed there but I managed to get into trouble again! The lady living next door but one to my grandparents was an invalid and I used to sit with her sometimes. Occasionally, I would get some shopping for her. One day, her son called in while I was there and he said to me if his mum asked me to buy any alcohol, I wasn't to get it. Well, this lady did ask me to get some, and said I was to take no notice of her son, he was just being silly and thought she was spending too much money. I was in a dilemma, what was I to do. Believe it or not, but I had not heard of alcoholics then, but looking back, I think this lady must have been one.

Anyway, I did get her some drink, I think it was a bottle of sherry and her son found out. Oh my goodness, was he cross. I felt pretty bad about it afterwards. Oh well, another lesson learnt.

Sometimes, Shirley and I would be allowed to go to the Pleasure Gardens. These were very nice gardens, some under glass. There was an area on the way there that had swings and a roundabout, so we would stop there on the way back, after we had been to the gardens. Well, we knew we had a deadline to get back for tea. Grandma did like us to be on time.

On this particular day, we had stopped at the play area and I said it was time to go back for tea. Well, Shirley said she didn't want to go back yet, she was enjoying herself. I said we must go, she said no, not yet! Oh dear, we argued about it and I said if she didn't come with me I was going anyway! Shirley said 'go on then, I don't care'. So I did! Now bear in mind, Shirley was only eight at the time.

Anyway, I stormed off and got halfway home when I started to have visions of somebody taking Shirley away, and imagined all sorts of things happening to her. I loved her lots really and got very worried. So I ran back so fast and nearly cried to see her swinging merrily away, not a care in the world. I think she must have seen my face, because she came running to me and we went home.

Soon it would be time to go back to Mum and Dad, our new home, and a new life.

One thing I loved to do when we stayed in Rhyl, was go to Splash Point. Now I have no idea what it is like there nowadays, because this was a long while ago. When I used to go, it was a bit sticking out into the sea with railings around it, and the name speaks for itself. If it was a bit wild and windy out, that was the best time. The waves would come up so high and I found it so exhilarating. I absolutely loved it there.

Grandma wasn't very happy about me going there on my own, but Grandad stuck up for me and said I would be fine. So every chance I got, off I would go. It was about ten minutes walk from my grandparents home and a lot of the time, I would run there. I have always loved the sea, and that is one of the things about living where I do nowadays. I am nowhere near the sea. I do however have the river Thames on my doorstep, but you don't see waves coming as high as I used to see at Splash Point. Maybe I will go on holiday to Rhyl sometime, just to see Splash Point.

Even though my grandparents were quite strict, they were never unreasonable and I did love staying with them.

Thirty Four

So now we start a new life here
The end of my tales is drawing near
We're in Maidenhead and it seems fine
Except for the school that will be mine

I will soon have a job and go to work
And I can tell you I will not shirk
When it comes I am put to the test
I really will try to do my best............

So we arrived in Maidenhead. I really wanted this to be the last move now and went to view our new home with excitement. It was a 3 bed roomed semi with front and back gardens. We hadn't lived anywhere so nice since we left Loughborough but at the moment as it was all new there, a new road and new houses, the workmen were still finishing some of the houses and the road was still a muddy track.

No matter, I loved it. I asked Mum and Dad could we please name the house Anchorage to show it will be our last home. They both agreed and so the house was named. I went back down that road recently and it is still called Anchorage although we long since left it behind.

While we were staying at Grandma and Grandad's in Rhyl, I used some of the time there to make cushion covers for our new three piece suite Mum had written about. Grandma had taught me to crochet and I made cushions out of different coloured wool and stitched some material Grandma gave me on the back. Mum was very pleased with them and put them on the cushions straight away.

Shirley and I had a bedroom each which was nice as we hadn't always had this luxury. It would be a long while before the garden would be nice, because of the workmen still around and it was all muddy. Dad said as soon as it was possible he would get to work on it.

I had to go and explore our new surroundings and set off to walk down the road and see where it led. Not very far away, I discovered Maidenhead Thicket. This was a marvellous place, full of trees and green areas and very big. In years to come, this was to be spoilt by having the M4 motorway through the middle of it. However, that was in the distant future and I was able to enjoy it as it was.

Maidenhead was much smaller than Leicester and everyone had a different accent. This is hardly noticed nowadays as people live and work in different places and accents are not so pronounced as they were then. I discovered there were two cinemas, the Rialto and the Plaza. The Rialto was the biggest and considered the posher one. It was quite common for teenagers to go to the Rialto and watch that film, then come out and go to the Plaza to watch the film there.

I took Shirley a couple of times to the Saturday morning club at the Rialto. This was where children could go and watch films specially for them. Once I was sure she would be ok, Shirley went on her own with some of her friends, so I didn't go any more as I was a bit old for this now.

Mum and Dad had got our schools all sorted out. I was to go to Boyn Hill Girls School and Shirley would go to Gordon Road. I was going to be learning French here at this new school. Unfortunately, I wasn't going to have very long learning it before I would be leaving school and going to work.

As you have now read, I went to quite a few different schools. Well, I enjoyed all of them in spite of moving around and some had different subjects, although obviously all had the basics the same. However, whether or not it was in my mind that I would be leaving in less than a year, but I couldn't seem to settle to this school. I think I felt I was biding my time, although I am sure I wasn't consciously aware of this.

I was ahead in some subjects and so got bored, but had not done French before and found it difficult to catch up. I also didn't like the dinners here and if I could, I would sneak off and run home to grab a sandwich there and then hurry back and join in as if I had been in the dining room! I was never found out!!

Even sport was limited here, and the netball team was full of girls who had been playing in the team for ages, so I wasn't needed there. All in all, I couldn't wait to leave and there were not even exams to do, as this was a secondary modern school and there were no exams to take. They were only at grammar schools, which if I hadn't said anything I would have been attending!

As the leaving date approached for my year, we had talks about what we would do when we left. There were discussions on our best options. There was also going to be someone from the Employment Exchange (this is now the Job Centre) to talk to us individually and find us suitable jobs to apply for.

Well, for some time now, I had decided I wanted to be a Nursery Nurse and bought a monthly magazine called Nursery Nurse and which advertised jobs. Lo and behold, I found a job I wanted and wrote to the Nursery. The job was for a Trainee nursery nurse and was in Egham which was some way away from Maidenhead. It would be a live in job and it was arranged for me to go for an interview. Mum and Dad were in two minds about this as I was only fifteen and to be leaving home at that age was a huge step.

We had a lot of chats about it and although not very happy, they could see how determined I was, so said they would think about it. Now the next thing that happened was a letter arrived from my Grandad Bramley in Rhyl. This was unusual in itself because as was so often the way, it was Grandma who always wrote letters for both of them.

Well, the point of the letter was for Mum and Dad to talk me out of going to live away from home. Grandad explained that he had to leave home at fourteen and didn't want the same things happening to me as had happened to him.

Do you know, all Mum and Dad had said to me about leaving, made no difference to me, I was still determined to go, but one letter from my Grandad and I wrote to the Nursery and said I wouldn't be going after all.

I think all of my family were very relieved.

So, what now? OK, what jobs are nearer to home, maybe I wouldn't be a nursery nurse after all. Mum did point out I would have my own little nursery when I got married and had babies.

I scoured the local newspapers, because I was going to get my own job and not be pushed into something by the school! Now I was really thinking about it, I thought maybe I will try office work. I had done some typing for Dad before, but I had no proper experience and had not had any lessons. Now that wasn't going to stop me.

Then I saw a job advertised at Vandervells nearby. This was a huge factory where they built bearings for racing cars. This factory was newly opened by Tony Vandervell and provided a lot of jobs for local people.

The job I was looking at was in the offices, not in the factory and I decided I would have a go at that. When I look back to that time, I am quite amazed at what I did! I cut the advertisement out of the paper and dressed in my best clothes, then off I went to Vandervells.

Well, when I got there, there was a guard on the gate and a long drive down to the factory, and you had to report to the guard before you could get in. The guard asked me what I wanted and I showed him the advertisement and said I was going for the job. He said had I got an appointment? Oh, goodness, I didn't think about that!! So naïve!! Luckily for me, the guard was very nice and he rang through to the office and explained about me. They told him to send me through! Oh now I was getting really nervous.

So off I went down this long drive and had to ask someone when I got to the end, as there were lots of doors and two different buildings. Eventually, I found my way there, and had an interview. In spite of having no experience and no certificates in typing or anything like that, and even the fact I hadn't yet left school, I still got the job!

I was to be working for Mr Evans. I am afraid I can't remember his job title. There were several senior secretaries and I would be helping them and learning at the same time and would have to deliver messages etc to other departments, sometimes in the factory. I would initially have to type address's on envelopes, all the while learning. Mr Evans was to review my progress in three months.

I was on cloud nine! The pay sounded good to me as well. I was due to start the first Monday after I left school. When I got home and told Mum and Dad they were absolutely gob smacked! I hadn't told them I was doing this, I just decided and went, telling nobody. However, once Mum and Dad had heard all the details etc, they were very pleased with me.

Now I was looking forward to telling the teachers at school, and especially the lady from the Employment Exchange. That day came round all too soon and I was called into the Head's office.

Goodness me, when I walked in there was the Headmistress, Miss Mumford, the lady from the Employment Exchange and another person whose part in this I can't recall. Anyway, the lady from the Employment Exchange started to ask me what kind of job I would like. She had notes from my form teacher in from of her, I couldn't see what it said, but guessed it was her opinion on what would be suitable for me.

Of course, I then said that it was alright because I already had a job to go to, so they needn't trouble about me! Oh dear, anyone would have thought I was about to start world war three! 'But you can't do things like that' said one (don't remember which one), and they all started saying things. So I explained what the job entailed etc and they wanted to know how I got it. When I told them, that set them off again!!

They said they would have to get in touch with my parents. I really think they thought I was pulling the wool over their eyes! Apparently, no one had just 'swanned off' and got a job like that without their approval! By this time, I was getting really fed up. I had thought they would be pleased I had used my initiative, instead of all this disapproval.

When I got home that night and told my parents, Dad laughed and said not to worry he would sort it. He must have done because no more was said at school after that.

The day then dawned that was to be my last at school and believe me, I was not sorry. This was one school I had not liked at all.

So, the Monday morning came and off I went. My first working day of my life! I was so excited and not really nervous at all.

So we come to the end of my adventures while growing up, and yes, it was fun......

A new chapter now begins..................

2405702

Made in the USA